Praise for *Beyond Wellness*

"*Beyond Wellness* provides an emotionally and intellectually honest alternative for people who are seeking meaning beyond generic spirituality. As a religious scholar and certified yoga instructor, Liz Bucar is the perfect person to provide insight into the deeper meaning and purpose of popular wellness practices."

—Pooja Lakshmin, MD, psychiatrist and author of *Real Self-Care*

"There is such a need for this book, and Liz Bucar is the perfect person to write it as a leading scholar of popular religious practices and one of the most prominent practitioners and proponents of bringing scholarly expertise into public spaces. More than that, Bucar has a way of bringing herself into the narrative in a way that is at once incisive and inviting."

—Kristin Kobes Du Mez, *New York Times* bestselling author of *Jesus and John Wayne*

"Bucar turns the oft-repeated 'I'm spiritual but not religious' on its head, showing us in her characteristic engaging style that we ought not to throw the proverbial baby out with the bathwater. In fact, the data show that when we understand the ancient religious traditions behind many spiritual practices, we make them more meaningful, ethical, and effective."

—Dan McClellan, *New York Times* bestselling author of *The Bible Says So* and cohost of *Data Over Dogma*

"Without the understanding this book offers, yoga, meditation, fad diets, and psychedelics might make you feel better, Bucar argues, but they won't make you well. These practices, it turns out, work better if we go beyond just doing them to understanding where they come from, mining their roots in wisdom traditions and moral communities."

—Stephen Prothero, *New York Times* bestselling author of *Religious Literacy*

"This book is bound to become an essential read for anyone taking their spirituality, health, and wellness seriously."

—Simran Jeet Singh, national bestselling author of *The Light We Give: How Sikh Wisdom Can Transform Your Life*

"The 'spiritual but not religious' movement is everywhere, often tied to promises of not just happiness but inner and outer well-being. Bucar moves through the claims of these ubiquitous movements not as a cynic but as one who cares enough to critique. This is a book that deserves the widest readership."

—Omid Safi, author of *Radical Love: Teachings from the Islamic Mystical Tradition*

"Consider this the next time you hear someone describe themselves as 'spiritual but not religious.' As Liz Bucar reminds us in *Beyond Wellness*, nearly every new meditation technique or holistic practice sold in today's spiritual marketplace is actually borrowed from one of those stodgy old religions these seekers think they left behind. Stripping those spiritual practices from their religious context, she argues, may even be hazardous to their own well-being."

—Don Lattin, national bestselling author of *The Harvard Psychedelic Club*

"If the spiritual salad bar has started to feel like quick dopamine with thin nutrition, this book offers substance. Read it if you want your spiritual practice to do more than lower your stress. Bucar has absolutely changed the way that I approach spiritual traditions."

—Britt Hartley, atheist spiritual director and author of *No Nonsense Spirituality*

"Thoughtfully breaking down the slippery realm of 'spirituality,' Bucar illuminates how all of these secular products and practices are historically rooted in religion, how they have been stripped of this context, and why that deracination serves no one. Rigorous and fun—just like Bucar's dispatches on TikTok—*Beyond Wellness* is a book we sorely need."

—Natalia Mehlman Petrzela, author of *Fit Nation* and host of *Welcome to Your Fantasy*

"I'm fond of saying religion is always in the room, and this book proves my point. We are living through a crisis that centers 'me' over 'we.' Mass-market mystics capitalize on this polarizing way of living, to our detriment. Bucar gets at the heart of this with her accessible scholarship and engaging analysis. This book reminds us that as humans we will never be able to be fully divorced from our need for meaning-making systems."

—Liz Kineke, writer, TV producer, and journalist

Also by Liz Bucar

Creative Conformity

Pious Fashion

Stealing My Religion

Beyond Wellness

HOW RESTORING THE RELIGIOUS ROOTS OF SPIRITUAL PRACTICES CAN HEAL US

Liz Bucar

TARCHER
an imprint of Penguin Random House
New York

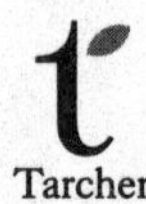

Tarcher
an imprint of Penguin Random House LLC
1745 Broadway, New York, NY 10019
penguinrandomhouse.com

Book design by Shannon Nicole Plunkett

LIBRARY OF CONGRESS CATALOGING-IN-PUBLICATION DATA

Names: Bucar, Elizabeth M., author.
Title: Beyond wellness: how restoring the religious roots of spiritual practices can heal us / Liz Bucar.
Description: New York: Tarcher, an imprint of Penguin Random House, [2026] | Includes bibliographical references and index.
Identifiers: LCCN 2025029250 (print) | LCCN 2025029251 (ebook) | ISBN 9780593854976 hardcover | ISBN 9780593854983 ebook
Subjects: LCSH: Health—Religious aspects | Healing—Religious aspects
Classification: LCC BL65.M4 B83 2026 (print) | LCC BL65.M4 (ebook) | DDC 204/.4—dc23/eng/20251203
LC record available at https://lccn.loc.gov/2025029250
LC ebook record available at https://lccn.loc.gov/2025029251

Printed in the United States of America
1st Printing

The authorized representative in the EU for product safety and compliance is Penguin Random House Ireland, Morrison Chambers, 32 Nassau Street, Dublin D02 YH68, Ireland, https://eu-contact.penguin.ie.

For Zoe

Full of life, loud joy, and unstoppable energy.
My greatest teacher and my best friend—
even if I'm not yours (yet).

This one's for you.

If we take the world's enduring religions at their best, we discover the distilled wisdom of the human race.

—HUSTON SMITH

Contents

Introduction

Why the Spiritual Salad Bar Isn't Serving Us

Oprah's daytime talk show that I watched as a teenager. The nineteenth-century transcendentalists I slogged through in graduate school. Pricey elixirs being marketed by Gwyneth Paltrow's company Goop on my Instagram feed. All have tried to convince me spirituality can exist without religion. And for a while I was on board. I thought I could access the benefits of spirituality through products, celebrity examples, and life hacks without getting involved in the messiness of religion.

But now I'm convinced these intellectuals and wellness influencers got it all wrong. Spiritual practices like yoga, mindfulness meditation, and plant psychedelics don't come from nowhere. They are associated with actual religious histories, systems of values, and communities quite often built and shaped over thousands of years. They work not because they are vaguely ancient or magical or mystical but because they have tapped into tried-and-true bodies of wisdom found in religious traditions.

And that makes me wonder: If we ignore the religious context and content of our spiritual techniques, are they missing their special sauce? Could they be even more powerful if we added the religion back in? Is there a way to do so without joining a religious community or declaring a religious identity?

I don't have a religious affiliation, but for twenty-five years, I have been a scholar, teacher, and student of religion. I was originally drawn to the study of religion while working on human rights issues after college, when it became clear that religious literacy was important just for understanding what the heck was going on. From civil rights to health care to nationalism, religious ideas, leaders, and institutions shape our world. So off to graduate school I went, earning a master's and doctorate from the University of Chicago Divinity School. I am currently a professor of religion at Northeastern University, where I teach popular classes like Selling Spirituality (which you'll hear more about later). The author of several books, I also write regularly about religion for mainstream media outlets and post educational content about religion on social media.

Although my original intention was to study religion as a way to understand how it shapes our political and social institutions, something much more personal—and unexpected—has happened as well. It has helped me understand my own commitments to well-being, even offering ways to shape or enrich them.

So here is my challenge to you. Consider that your favorite spiritual self-care technique is probably a knockoff of a religious one. You gain from that extraction a sense of control, but something important is also lost—ethical frameworks, long-term commitments to a community, systemic understanding of suffering and sickness, insights into human nature, and more. By taking the religion behind that practice a bit more seriously, you might land on a version of a spiritual/religious mash-up that is better for your well-being and the well-being of others.

Not so fast, you might be thinking. *I'm no fan of institutionalized religion.* And I get it. Religion has a PR problem, and for good reason. Religious institutions have protected abusive clergy, instilled sexist and racist policies, supported narrow interpretations of sacred texts, condemned queerness, and exacerbated prejudice. They have been on the front lines of the most polarizing political battles of my lifetime, such as regulating sexuality, denying access to health care services, fighting over borders, and framing religious minorities as the dangerous "other." For many people in the fast-growing religiously unaffiliated demographic known as the "nones"—and yes, I'm part of this group—the organized religion of our parents' and grandparents' generations seems too outdated, conservative, and restrictive to add meaning to our lives.

But we don't have to throw out the baby with the bathwater. We don't have to reject all religious ideas and values just because religious institutions have done us and others wrong. Religious communities, scholars, and leaders have grappled with what a good human life looks like for a long, long time, and their insights can be useful even for those of us who aren't comfortable with claiming a religious identity.

Religious communities, scholars, and leaders have grappled with what a good human life looks like for a long, long time, and their insights can be useful even for the nonreligious.

And the truth is that many of us who think we have given up on religion haven't distanced ourselves as much as we might think. We exist in a muddy area between organized religion and secularism, unchurched but religiously curious. Instead of ordering a meal off the menu—instead of becoming, say, a Presbyterian, Reform Jew, or Zen Buddhist—we treat religious traditions as a spiritual salad bar, filling our plates with our favorite items in a constant search for the perfect combo.

But rather than making us better, I suspect popular spiritual practices are functioning like dopamine hits that prevent us from putting in the hard work necessary to live fully ethical, relational, and sustainable lives. A yoga retreat is a temporary Band-Aid on the stress of work deadlines, carpools, and family drama. The endorphins I get from spiritual fitness classes only last an hour. Detox diets are poisoning my relationship with food. I worry the spiritual practices I'm drawn to are extracted from religious minorities and thus out me as a Becky or maybe even a Karen. It's not the picking and choosing from the spiritual salad bar that gives me pause—it's the fact that we've stopped caring about what's in each ingredient. In our search for the perfect mash-up of spiritual therapies, we're adopting practices without understanding their religious associations.

I don't want us to give up spiritual practices. I want them to work better. No matter what you've been told, there's a way to engage with the religious substance of popular spiritual techniques with more knowledge and depth without becoming "churched." Reconnecting our spiritual practices to religion allows these practices to be more meaningful, more responsible, and more effective. Showing you how is what this book is about.

Each chapter chronicles my search for the religious essence of a popular wellness practice including yoga, mindfulness meditation, Alcoholics Anonymous meetings, spiritual fitness classes, detox diets, sound baths, and plant psychedelics. Many of these practices will be familiar to you. You have probably tried one or two yourself. But even if they're not your cup of tea, their popularity points to something that might be valuable to you. You don't have to believe wholesale in a religion to understand it has wisdom to offer.

Think of this book as a guide for walking a path between dogmatic religion and bland spirituality in a three-step process.

Step one: Learn how the religion of a given spiritual practice was hidden from us in the first place. It turns out the belief that a practice is "spiritual but not religious" often depends on erasing key aspects of religious history. Sometimes the process of extraction is exploitative. Often it involves the Christianization—specifically, the Protestantization—of non-Christian practices. In each case, we will figure out how we got to where we are today.

Step two: Restore the religion to a spiritual practice by reconnecting it to its traditional meaning and communities. Think of those religious associations as the missing ingredients at the spiritual salad bar. But don't confuse unearthing religious roots to mean we are returning to some "original" form of practice, like monastic mindfulness or premodern psychedelic rituals. I know there's a temptation to find some "pure" form of a practice, uncorrupted by history or culture. But that isn't how religions work. They aren't simple repositories of unchanging practices and beliefs. Better to think of them as resources—modes of interpretation, conceptual frameworks, communities of support—for how to make life better or fuller.

Step three: Apply these religious insights to our lives. This is not a one-size-fits-all solution. What we do with our newfound religious knowledge depends on who we are and our core values. For example, I have come to see my yoga practice as a way I train myself to be a better person, not just cultivate physical flexibility or emotional resilience. Similarly, noticing that I'm drawn to group spiritual exercise classes made it clear that, for me, the role of a community is just as important to my post-class endorphin high as raising my heart rate. While I don't have a problem with substance abuse, I found that Alcoholics Anonymous's understanding of a higher power offers me a way to think about how all my attempts to fix, manage, and control my life are patterns of "God play," and thus doomed to fail. And sacramental use of psychedelics helped me come to terms with my father's death.

These are just some of the ways I learned to apply religion to my mostly nonreligious life while taking a deeper dive into the popular spiritual practices in this book. As you explore, you'll find your own ways to use religious insights to enhance your life that are unique to your life experience.

In fact, this book offers you something more than "wellness." Let's call it well-being. The wellness industry has convinced us wellness is an ideal BMI, glowing skin, or a positive attitude. But for thousands of years, religious thinkers and communities have grappled with the purpose and meaning of our lives in much more holistic terms. Moral characters, just societies, responsibility to your neighbor, a balanced relationship with nature—these are all markers of well-being. Taking these things seriously is how we achieve something beyond wellness.

This book also offers you something beyond spirituality. Something more than a random collection of personal therapy techniques. Something that asks more of you. Something that is engaged, challenging, and disruptive. Something that requires conviction, discipline, and community. And we already have a word for that. We call it religion.

1

Bendy Bodies

A SWEDISH ACTRESS, A NEW ENGLAND HOUSEWIFE, AND A CALIFORNIA LAWSUIT'S LESSONS FOR YOGA

I was on a yoga retreat at the Kripalu Center in the Berkshires the week the world changed. On Monday, March 9, 2020, rising COVID-19 infection rates in China and Italy dominated the news. On Wednesday, COVID-19 was declared a pandemic by the World Health Organization. On Thursday, there was a confirmed case of COVID-19 in my daughter's school, which was traced back to a parent who had attended a local Biogen conference that turned out to be a super-spreader event. On Friday, my father-in-law was exposed to COVID-19 in Canada and put into quarantine. Kripalu shut down on Saturday, March 14, and as I drove home, I formed a plan to use my yoga to deal with the unknowns of COVID-19.

But that didn't happen—at least not in the way I intended.

I had very little time to practice yoga postures those first few weeks of lockdown while trying to figure out how to teach college courses online, homeschool a sixth grader, and deal with a stressed-out partner. And yet, multiple times a day, I found myself returning to the religious systems and worldviews that gave rise to my yoga practice. *Vedanta*, which emphasizes impermanence of all things, helped me remember that this too shall pass. *Sankhya*, which teaches that we do not have control over external events, reminded me all I could do was try to control my reaction to what was happening. And *Tantra*, which views everyday experiences as a way to encounter the divine, reminded me to appreciate family, a sunny day, and a home-cooked meal.

These were all religious ideas I had internalized through engaging in yoga postures, and they were shaping my reaction to a world that was now more uncertain, scary, and dangerous. Yoga was functioning as a resource for resilience—but only because I was able to tap into its religious insights.

This chapter is not trying to convince you to give up your daily flow. I get it. You love yoga. Me too. I belong to a fancy studio. I occasionally vacation at yoga retreat centers. I'm even a certified yoga teacher. I wouldn't give up my yoga, so I'm not asking you to do so either. And yet, I think that the idea that yoga is not or should not be religious deserves some interrogation.

I know even suggesting yoga could be religious goes against the popular view. Most of my friends who regularly practice yoga know it has origins in South Asian devotional communities, but they have convinced themselves that *their* yoga is not religious—it's only spiritual, or maybe even completely secular. This is the type of yoga I want to discuss, the "wellness yoga" that has become so popular over the last twenty years, promising that its postures, deep breaths, and namastes will make us more toned, centered, and resilient. This type of yoga has been successfully reinvented. It's no longer a practice of religious devotion but one of self-care.

I can already hear my yoga friends' objections: *Liz, why would you try to add religion to something as fun and harmless as yoga?* But notice that objection assumes there is some problem with religion. It assumes that if yoga has some religious content, it is no longer safe or effective for most of us. But what if instead of associating religion with trauma, control, or toxicity, we gave it the benefit of the doubt? What if we considered the possibility that we are partly drawn to yoga *because* of its devotional meanings, not in spite of them? I know yoga started working better for me when I began to understand more of its religious content and context. What if the same can be true for you?

A PROBLEMATIC LEGAL RULING

In July 2013, a packed courtroom waited to hear the fate of the first district-wide public-school yoga program in the nation. Eighteen months earlier, the Encinitas Union School District (EUSD) had replaced much of its PE offerings for kindergarten through sixth grade with a yoga curriculum. Who needed dodgeball when yoga could build resilience without pummeling kids with a rubber ball? It seemed like a no-brainer—until the lawsuit.

Today, yoga is widely accepted as appropriate for secular settings. But can it really be nonreligious, or is that just a sleight of hand? This was the question at the center of *Sedlock v. Baird.* If yoga, even PE yoga, was religious, then the Encinitas program violated the First Amendment's guarantee of freedom of religion, much in the same way mandatory prayer in schools would. But if yoga was secular, or better yet, if the religion could be extracted from yoga, then the program was fine.

Encinitas, California, which is sometimes called "OM-cinitas," was an obvious location to pioneer a public-school yoga program. This wealthy coastal town in Southern California is known for excellent surfing and an outdoor lifestyle. It was dubbed "the healthiest place in America" way back in 1937 by Paramahansa Yogananda's Self-Realization Fellowship, which set up their headquarters there. Because the town prides itself on promoting wellness, yoga in local schools made sense to some civic leaders. It was a way to teach kids the importance of wellness early, by providing them techniques for taking personal responsibility for their health.

Encinitas is also ground zero for Ashtanga yoga, a form of yoga developed and popularized by K. Pattabhi Jois. Trained by the famous yogi Tirumalai Krishnamacharya in India, Jois (like many of Krishnamacharya's students) became an avid yoga evangelist, determined to spread yoga in America, where he arrived in 1975 and set up shop in an abandoned Episcopal church in Encinitas. His form of yoga, Ashtanga, links postures and breathing to create a dynamic sequence or "flow," referred to as *vinyasa*. It eventually became one of the most popular forms of yoga in the Western world, especially for those seeking a very physical and athletic practice.

Ashtanga yoga exhibits several characteristics that might be called religious. Its founder, Jois, traced his lineage to the god Shiva. It has a sacred language (Sanskrit) and sacred places, like Mysore, India, where many devotees hope to study at some point in their life. It has rituals.

It also has a comprehensive belief system that addresses the entire cycle of life. Ashtanga is named for the eight limbs laid out in Patanjali's Yoga Sutras (circa 400 CE), which are:

1. Yama (restraints)
2. Niyama (observances)
3. Asana (postures)
4. Pranayama (breath control)
5. Pratyahara (withdrawal of the senses)
6. Dharana (concentration)
7. Dhyana (meditation)
8. Samadhi (absorption)

These limbs provide guidance on how to attain not just inner peace but also a state of unity with the broader universe. For instance, the yama and niyama together form a system of values to guide moral living, and everything rests on beliefs about the nature of reality, including the existence of the divine.

The goal of Ashtanga yoga looks pretty religious too. Called *samadhi*, it is a state of profound awareness of the oneness of the universe, often described as experiencing the divine reality.

Finally, Ashtanga yoga has a proselytizing element, encouraging its devotees to teach others Ashtanga as a way of life. And that was the reason for its interest in public schools. Given Jois's roots in Encinitas, it made sense that the KP Jois Foundation would begin a yoga-in-school campaign with the local school district. And they even footed the bill with a $533,000 grant for the program.

But it wasn't smooth sailing. In addition to surfers and yogis, Encinitas has an evangelical population and a very active chapter of Moms in Prayer that holds weekly prayer meetings for the school staff, teachers, and children. And it was the leader of this group, Jennifer Sedlock, along with her husband and a conservative attorney, who would eventually bring a lawsuit against the EUSD for its yoga program.

Sedlock was living in Encinitas in 2012 when she learned that her children's school, El Camino Creek Elementary, was starting a new yoga initiative at a back-to-school night. The principal didn't give many details about the program, but according to Sedlock's book, *The Yoga Crisis in America*, when she did a little digging, she learned yoga would replace sixty of the one hundred minutes of mandatory physical education each week and was supported by a grant from what she characterizes as "a highly religious organization that only taught and promoted 'Ashtanga' yoga." Sedlock became even more concerned after she observed a yoga demonstration.

She wasn't the only one. Some parents thought the prostration to a non-Judeo-Christian god during a sun salutation smacked of idolatry. Other parents worried yoga exposed their children to harmful spirits. Others were just plain suspicious of Asian forms of religious practice. And to many parents, yoga in schools felt like a form of religious instruction, one that undermined their authority by indoctrinating their children with beliefs contrary to their own. It felt like yoga was coming for their children, proselytizing right under their noses.

Several parents met to discuss their concerns in the fall of 2012. They collected 250 signatures from community members who wanted the yoga program suspended and brought their concerns to four school board meetings. The school district refused to budge.

And that was when Dean Broyles got involved. Broyles, a local attorney, is president of the National Center for Law &

Policy, a legal defense organization which "focuses on the protection and promotion of religious freedom, the sanctity of life, traditional marriage, parental rights, and other civil liberties." He advised the concerned parents that a lawsuit would get the school board to respond. The Sedlocks volunteered to be named as plaintiffs. Broyles filed a complaint in February 2013 on their behalf claiming EUSD's yoga program "unlawfully promotes religious beliefs, while disfavoring and discriminating against other religions." The central question of the lawsuit was whether EUSD's yoga was religious and thus in violation of the religious freedom protections of the First Amendment of the Constitution. The school district said no. The Sedlocks said yes.

Originally scheduled as a two-hour bench trial, the proceedings of *Sedlock v. Baird* ultimately took seven days. It turned out deciding if yoga was religious was far more complicated than the court had anticipated.

The Honorable John S. Meyer was the trial judge for *Sedlock v. Baird*, and his decision is cited as legal precedent for the idea that yoga is secular. But that is not exactly what he ruled. Meyer actually found that "yoga is religious" and specified that Ashtanga yoga has "religious roots in Hindu, Buddhist, and other metaphysical religious practice." And, although Meyer agreed that the yoga program at EUSD was based on Ashtanga yoga, he decided the school district had sufficiently remade yoga to be "completely devoid of any religious, mystical, or spiritual trappings." Put simply, according to Judge Meyer, yoga itself might be religious, but the EUSD yoga program was not, making it exempt from First Amendment concerns about religion.

Judge Meyer's Ruling

The following excerpts from Judge Meyer's ruling in *Sedlock v. Baird* illuminate the tension within the conception of yoga as simultaneously religious and secular:

- "We assume, without deciding, that Ashtanga yoga, insofar as it prescribes the practice of an eight-limbed form of yoga in which the eighth and final limb is 'union with the universal or the divine,' is a religion for purposes of the establishment clause of the California Constitution."
- "A reasonable observer would not conclude that the District is engaged in religious activity merely because teachers directed the children to perform poses that some individuals consider to have religious significance."
- "While the practice of yoga may be religious in some contexts, yoga classes as taught in the District are, as the trial court determined, 'devoid of any religious, mystical, or spiritual trappings.'"

Foundational to Meyer's decision was his understanding that religion is primarily about beliefs. For Meyer, and for millions of Americans, Ashtanga yoga is religious not because of the postures themselves but rather because of the theological meanings the Ashtanga practitioner ascribes to them. Meyer accepted the EUSD argument that they had successfully erased these religious meanings by, for example, renaming postures with English names: "opening sequences" instead of sun salutations, "crisscross applesauce" instead of lotus pose. Meyer went as far as to say that a "reasonable student" would not perceive that EUSD yoga advances religion. The religious problem, it turned out, was not the practice, but any individual whose understanding of religion did not prioritize belief above all else.

Yet the reduction of religion to just beliefs is something folks who study religion for a living reject. In fact, the idea that religion is primarily about beliefs is a very Protestant view. One of the notable features of Protestantism, as distinct from Catholicism and other branches of Christianity, is the doctrine of *sola fide*, which states that believers are saved by faith alone. This is especially pronounced in American evangelicalism, which emphasizes believing very specific ideas in order to get into heaven. But in many other religious communities, practices are just as central as beliefs, if not more so. Practices can create commitments to dogma, display a submission to a god or gods, cultivate specific character traits, or orient the believer in the world. So if the practices of yoga are religious, the removal of that religion might not be as easy as Meyer thought.

You don't have to take just my word for it. Candy Gunther Brown, a religion professor who served as an expert witness for the plaintiffs in *Sedlock v. Baird*, makes this same point in her book *Debating Yoga and Mindfulness in Public Schools*. She is critical of Meyer's decision on several grounds, including his rather anemic understanding of yoga and religion. She writes, "Ashtanga is grounded in experiential, rather than doctrinal, assumptions about the relationship between beliefs and practices: Sun salutations and lotus are *embodied prayers* that do not depend on linguistic framing or practitioner intentions to *instill* beliefs or (presumably) effect spiritual change." If Brown is correct that yoga postures are embodied religious practices, simply renaming them "crisscross applesauce" wouldn't make them secular.

If the *Sedlock v. Baird* trial proved anything about religion, it is that the "spiritual but not religious" mindset depends on a lack of religious literacy, especially when it comes to Eastern religions. Brown suggests a helpful analogy: EUSD would not have allowed teachers to have students make the Catholic sign of the cross, even if they renamed it "a zigzag" and said it was a warm-up for cursive lessons. The difference, Brown points out, is that Catholic rituals of devotion are more familiar to most Americans than the ones associated with yoga.

Take the common yoga pose chaturanga dandasana—in which the body is held parallel to the ground by the balls of feet and palms, elbows bent. Many Americans experience this pose as a challenging low "plank" useful for building core strength and practicing remaining calm under stressful conditions. But as religious studies scholar Amanda Lucia explains in her book *White Utopias*, this posture developed within a prostration culture, in which holding your body parallel to the earth was an act of submission to the divine. So many Americans read chaturanga as merely a plank because of a lack of understanding of that other cultural and religious context. It's not that the religious meaning is not there; it's that many of us—including Judge Meyer—don't know it.

Before we get into the specifics of how we can benefit from approaching yoga in a religious way, let's figure out how yoga came to be dissociated from religion in the first place. Because this was certainly not always the case. And the story of how we got here features a Swedish actress and a New England housewife.

THE FIRST LADIES OF WELLNESS YOGA

Yoga historically includes a wide range of devotional techniques, made up of hundreds of lineages originating in South Asia, preserved and promoted by thousands of gurus all claiming authority and expertise. But within a hundred years of arriving in the United States, Americans changed all that. Today when I ask, "What is yoga?," most folks answer something about stretching that reduces personal stress. While some think yoga is indebted to the religions of South Asia—in fact, that's part of its appeal—most don't think it's religious per se. Instead they see it primarily as a form of self-care—that it is, as the common phrase goes, "spiritual but not religious."

Many people helped popularize this understanding of yoga in the United States during the twentieth century, and you may have heard of some of the most famous ones: Paramahansa Yogananda and K. Pattabhi Jois, whom I've already mentioned, and also Swami Vivekananda, B. K. S. Iyengar, and Bikram Choudhury. But two Western women also played a pivotal role in the framing of yoga as a universal wellness technique: Indra Devi and Lilias Folan. Both Devi and Folan practiced devotional yoga themselves, but they promised their students yoga did not need to come with that baggage. These women were both called the "first lady of yoga" at the height of their popularity. They gave us permission to leave behind the complicated systems of thought that made us uncomfortable and borrow just enough Asian aesthetics to make us believe we had discovered a path to wellness developed by sages in faraway lands.

Indra Devi Brings Yoga to Hollywood

If you—like me—are a white woman who practices yoga, Indra Devi paved the way for you. She was born Eugenie Peterson in 1899 in Latvia, to a Russian noble mother and a Swedish banker father. After the Bolshevik Revolution of 1917, she and her mother left Moscow for Berlin, where Eugenie became an actress and dancer, touring throughout Europe. At the age of twenty-eight, she moved to India, took the stage name Indra Devi, and quickly became a rising star in Indian films.

In 1930, Devi married a Czech diplomat posted to India, and it was through him she met the maharaja of Mysore, who supported Sri Krishnamacharya's famous yoga school. At the time, yoga was almost an exclusively male pursuit, and when Devi asked to study with Krishnamacharya, he initially refused. But Devi persisted and eventually convinced the yogi to take her on as his first female student. She would go on to become the first Westerner to teach yoga in India.

In 1947, just after the death of her husband, Devi brought her stage presence, teaching experience, and collection of saris to California to introduce yoga to America's rich and famous. She knew it wouldn't be easy to promote yoga in America, but she had a plan. Although she had been trained by Krishnamacharya in the full range of devotional yoga practices, Devi only taught postures and breathing techniques to her American clients—no confusing foreign metaphysics, ethical systems, or cosmologies required. Devi also leveraged Americans' growing interest in wellness by framing yoga as therapeutic, a practice that could provide longevity and vitality.

And then there was Devi herself. She was trained in India by a guru and dressed in Indian garb, so she was authentically exotic. She was also an attractive Western woman and thus relatable to her white, mostly female clients. If yoga was pretty, feminine, blue-eyed, and Swedish, just how dangerous could it be? She cultivated an exclusive clientele of Hollywood stars, including Gloria Swanson and Greta Garbo, which helped make yoga aspirational to ordinary Americans.

Devi extended the influence of her yoga teaching beyond her famous students by writing two books. *Forever Young, Forever Healthy* came out in 1953 and offered yoga as a simple self-care technique capable of warding off illness and aging. Devi understood that pared-down wellness yoga was less likely to offend her audience than rigorous devotional yoga. And she was right. The book became a bestseller.

Devi understood that pared-down wellness yoga was less likely to offend her audience than rigorous devotional yoga. And she was right.

Her second book, *Yoga for Americans*, was published in 1959 as a more detailed guide for home yoga practice. This time Devi gave her readers a bit more Orientalist content—there was an om symbol on the cover of the book and some description of nadis and chakras—but the six-week course of yoga was still presented as accessible to anyone. "It will help businessmen and sportsmen, public speakers, models and housewives," she wrote, decades before corporate and community yoga programs existed. *Yoga for Americans* was another bestseller, and after it was published, Devi picked up the title "first lady of yoga."

Lilias Folan Makes Yoga as American as Apple Pie

Devi's approach to yoga was an important step to helping American yoga become something that would eventually be considered safe enough for public schools. But we weren't there yet, because as postural yoga became more popular in the 1960s, it began to be tied to new religious movements, and that put its acceptability to mainstream Americans, especially Protestant Americans, at risk.

Take the International Society for Krishna Consciousness (ISKCON), popularly known as the Hare Krishna movement. The story of Hare Krishnas in America began in 1966 when A. C. Bhaktivedanta Swami Prabhupada came to New York and established a countercultural community. The movement appealed to a younger generation of mostly white hippies who were interested in disrupting society through practices like a vegetarian diet, dress codes, a monastic lifestyle, and, yes, yoga. One of the first places Swami Prabhupada operated out of was a yoga studio, and he made yoga one of the community's central devotional practices. At the same time, Indian swamis like Satchidananda Saraswati and Amrit Desai were establishing yoga-focused ashrams in the United States, specifically Yogaville and Kripalu.

We were back to square one: Yoga was associated with religion. This meant American Christian white ladies again needed someone to convince them yoga was a wellness technique that could be safely practiced without submitting to religious dogma or joining a cult. They needed someone who could convince them that the essence of yoga was self-care and that this essence was independent of its devotional origins or new religious manifestations.

Enter our second "first lady of yoga," Lilias Folan, who

would introduce yoga to millions of Americans through her show on PBS from 1974 to 1999. My mom was one of her early fans.

Born in Pennsylvania in 1947, my mom was a cheerleader in high school and majored in home economics at Penn State, where she met my father. She taught high school home ec for a few years, and then became a stay-at-home mother, eventually to three girls. All of this is to say my mother led a fairly traditional life. The yoga of countercultural religious movements would not have been her vibe.

But shortly after I was born, my mom discovered yoga, like so many Americans in the 1970s, from Lilias Folan's public television show. She was so taken by Folan's yoga program that she went on to teach yoga herself at churches, community centers, and, for a short stint, the University of New Hampshire. Today, in her late seventies, she still does yoga daily, preferring to practice on braided rugs over the fancy yoga mat I purchased for her. My mom is very active in her local Lutheran church, and she does not consider her yoga religious. She is confident yoga requires no devotion to any Eastern religious beliefs. Folan was the one who convinced her this was the case.

Like my mom, Folan was a housewife and mother. She started attending yoga classes in 1964 at the Stamford, Connecticut, YMCA to deal with mild depression. Once she experienced the healing power of yoga—which she credits with curing her general malaise—Folan saw teaching yoga to others as her calling.

When one of her students whose husband was a producer at Cincinnati's public television station, WCET, suggested Folan pitch a yoga show, she was intrigued. But Folan faced a challenge if she wanted to convince producers yoga was appropriate for public television. The idea that yoga was not religious was no longer an easy sell. In the 1970s, yoga in America *was* considered religious—at least, some yoga was—so Folan had to show WCET that her yoga wasn't. It is rather extraordinary that she succeeded.

Like Devi, Folan was no stranger to religious forms of yoga. She studied yoga with masters like Iyengar (who was trained by Devi's guru) and Swami Chidananda Saraswati Maharaj of the Divine Life Society ashram. In 1998, Goswami Kriyananda gave her the title Swami Kavitananda, "one who knows bliss through energy, movement, and poetry." But by the time she started talks with WCET, she had figured out it was best to leave most of what she knew about the devotional meanings of yoga behind when teaching other housewives. To them she was no swami, just Lilias, an approachable mom in her thirties who looked good in a leotard. Someone who had knowledge of ancient spiritual techniques, but wasn't a hippie or otherwise spreading dangerous countercultural ideas. As *Time* magazine put it, "Lilias promises to become the Julia Child of yoga," translating a foreign cuisine for the American palate.

Folan's PBS show, *Lilias, Yoga and You*, first aired in 1970 on WCET and within three years was broadcast nationally by PBS, where it ran until 1999. The format was simple. Folan appeared on a carpeted platform, her long brown hair braided, wearing a full-body leotard with a racing stripe down each side and an om symbol on the chest. She began with a little chat about banishing negative thoughts or how to successfully diet, sharing her own experiences of self-transformation. And then she cheerfully led a series of yoga postures by breaking each pose down into easy-to-follow segments and explaining their specific health benefits, whether related to digestion, releasing tension, or stretching a specific muscle.

And while Folan's yoga was not religious and required no religious commitments, Eastern spirituality was the inspiration for its aesthetics. Her show opens with the program's name in a stylized font that is obviously meant to read as exotic and Oriental. Folan sometimes uses the Sanskrit names for poses, so you might expect the font to look like Sanskrit, but it is more reminiscent of Arabic script, perhaps to avoid association with the yoga texts that would have been popular with the new religious movements of the time. I call this "yoga font"—vaguely spiritual and Eastern, but not tied to any specific religion or location. It evokes just enough otherness to be intriguing to a white Protestant American audience, to whom all Eastern aesthetics are interchangeable.

Folan published several yoga books, including *Lilias, Yoga and You* (1972), *Lilias, Yoga, and Your Life* (1981), *Lilias! Yoga Gets Better with Age* (2005), and *Lilias! Yoga: Your Guide to Enhancing Body, Mind, and Spirit in Midlife and Beyond* (2011). Folan offered her readers gentle postures, supported holds, breath work to calm the nervous system, and affirming meditations to quiet the mind, reduce stress, and achieve personal health. She presented yoga as part of a wellness routine.

The spiritualty of Folan's yoga was part of its power, but that spirituality was so vague the student got to define it in any way she wanted. Take the example of Folan's use of the word *namaste* to end her classes. Scholars are not sure exactly when namaste began to be used in yoga instruction, but today it is a common way to end a yoga class. Solemnly, reverently, hands pressed together at the heart's center, often with a bow of gratitude, we chant namaste to seal our practice. Never mind that in South Asia, the word is used as a greeting, so to close a yoga class with it is like ending with "hello." To our untrained Western ears, a "yoga namaste" sounds spiritual and yet not religious. It adds acoustic gravitas to a yoga class but only through linguistic window dressing, much like the "yoga font" of Folan's program.

About 10 percent of Americans practice yoga today, and most have had to be convinced that yoga is not religious, or at least not religious in an Eastern way, to do so. A 2022 Yoga Alliance survey found that 73 percent of American respondents don't even think yoga is spiritual. The most popular reason for practicing yoga? Reduction of stress (51 percent) and increased flexibility (46 percent).

Devi and Folan are why. While both were familiar with devotional yoga, they helped develop and then teach thousands of Americans wellness yoga. This yoga sprinkled on just enough Asian spice—saris, leotards with om symbols, yoga font, a namaste—to make it feel like an ancient Eastern technique. But it required no understanding of complicated religious metaphysics, cosmologies, or values. The yoga these women offered was a health tonic meant to cure the stress of modern life for everyone from Hollywood starlets to housewives. It was especially safe when learned from blue-eyed Swedes or attractive New Englanders. It was even educational. PBS said so.

Although as a religious studies scholar, I should have known better, I took a similar approach the first time I taught yoga on my campus shortly after getting certified to do so. I had studied devotional yoga on my own, and it was part of my yoga teacher training, but I tried to offer a secular class. I used English names for postures. I did not utter a single om. I did not mention Brahman or the divine, or any other explicitly religious terminology. I didn't quote the Bhagavad Gita or Yoga Sutras. I left my mala beads at home.

When I think back on those choices, it occurs to me that when I scrubbed my class of Eastern words, gestures, and beliefs, it was because I had presumed, much like Judge Meyer, that the religion of yoga was in its associated linguistic trappings and philosophical beliefs. I forgot what I know all too well, namely that embodied practices themselves are central to how religious communities reinforce and even create beliefs.

But there was something else at play. I had also bought into Devi and Folan's idea that yoga practices were somehow "safe" as techniques of self-care only when dereligioned, reinforcing the idea that religion, especially Eastern religion, was somehow too dangerous for my Boston-based students. I had become a promoter of a form of spiritual wellness that reinforces the hierarchy of the superior "individual spiritual seeker" and an inferior "religious subject or community."

RESTORING RELIGION TO YOGA

I'm a fan of yoga. I'm just convinced we have been duped into thinking that yoga is something less substantial than it could be. When we let yoga advocates reduce yoga to a form of personal self-care (I'm looking at you, first ladies of yoga) or present it as something easily extracted from its religious contexts with a few linguistic substitutions (now I'm looking at you, Judge Meyer), we're missing out on the potential of this practice to contribute more deeply to our understanding of well-being and the well-being of others.

Yoga does not belong to one religion. It is more accurate to say it developed within and alongside several religious traditions, including Hinduism, Buddhism, Jainism, and Sikhism. And then there are various schools and lineages of yoga, each with its own honored teachers and specific practices. All this diversity means there are many ways to approach learning more about yoga's devotional associations.

The first step is to stop insisting yoga can't be religious or that only its nonreligious forms are safe for mainstream consumption. Once we're open to the idea that yoga might have devotional meanings that can contribute to our understanding of real well-being, we realize it can do a lot more than tone our butts or teach us techniques of emotional self-regulation.

One of yoga's biggest insights into well-being is about the power of somatic, or embodied, practices. In the United States, the culturally dominant view of the body is that it is controlled by the mind. This might seem like a secular perspective, and in some ways it is, but in many ways it's actually a very Christian way of thinking about the body. In fact, one way to describe Christianity, especially Protestant Christianity, is that it emphasizes *orthodoxy*, or right belief. Other religions, such as Judaism and Islam, but also the Asian religious traditions that yoga developed alongside, could be described as emphasizing *orthopraxy*, or right practice. In an orthopractic framing, somatic rituals don't just convey fidelity to beliefs, they are also the mechanisms for creating those beliefs.

Put simply, the insight here is that the things we physically do with our bodies can change us. This is one reason I think it is important to understand the religious contexts our wellness practices are often plucked from—those contexts might be affecting us, even without our knowing. They are among the ingredients missing from the spiritual salad bar.

The religious contexts our wellness practices are plucked from might be affecting us without our even knowing.

Let's look a bit closer at how the role of somatic practices is described in some forms of devotional yoga. For instance, K. Pattabhi Jois, the founder of the Ashtanga yoga that was the basis of the controversial EUSD yoga program, thought yoga was embodied religion aimed at understanding divinity. More specifically, Jois believed yoga asanas could instill ideas to help us get closer to what he saw as our goal: a state of consciousness called samadhi, in which we become one with the divine. In fact, Jois once told an interviewer that anyone who practices yoga postures would come to "experience God inside . . . whether they want it or not." Many Ashtanga students and teachers don't know the extent of Jois's religious orientation because, like Devi and Folan, he underplayed it to make yoga more appealing to Americans. But Jois thought the somatic practices of yoga did imprint religious understandings on us.

I am certified to teach Kripalu yoga, and in this lineage, postural practice is described as the way to access "body wisdom" through the direct experience of the ultimate source of authority. "The keystone teaching of Kripalu yoga" according to Richard Faulds, past president and CEO of the Kripalu Center, "is a call for each individual to use the techniques of yoga to access the innate evolutionary intelligence lying dormant in the body." During teacher training, my instructors emphasized ancient sources associated with yoga that establish a metaphysical basis for the power of embodied practices.

Take Tantric philosophy, which dates to about 500 CE. At that time, it offered a departure from early systems of thought that saw the material world as separate from the sacred world—what philosophers call dualism. In contrast, the non-dualist Tantric view was that by experiencing the things in this world fully, rather than avoiding them, we access infinite reality. This allowed for a positive and powerful role for the body in religious practice. And I think this idea is at the heart of yoga: We can obtain spiritual health through body work.

If postures reinforce beliefs, what beliefs can or do your postures imprint on you? A lot of this depends on what type of yoga you practice and the beliefs of the community you practice with.

For Jois, yoga asanas are experiential forms of religion, instilling ideas to help us get closer to the divine. Let's look at the postures that bookend every one of Jois's Ashtanga flows, and consider how they function to help reach this devotional goal.

An Ashtanga sequence begins with sun salutations, also known as surya namaskar. A sun salutation includes bowing forward with hands in prayer position and a chaturanga in which the body is held parallel to the earth—which, as I mentioned earlier, in Indic prostration culture would be understood as an act of submission to the god of gods. For Jois, the purpose of this series of linked postures is clear. They are a way to worship the sun god, who contains the rest of the pantheon of Hindu gods. Jois's sun salutation comprises forms of physical submission meant to inspire an attitude of submission. The final pose in an Ashtanga flow is savasana, or corpse pose, in which we lie on our backs, legs and arms splayed out, completely still. Jois sees this posture as an invitation to think about our own impending death and the symbolic death of the ego. The result might give us a renewed sense of purpose by putting things in perspective so that we are inspired to make good use of our time. We could say that two key religious ideas reinforced by the opening and closing postures of Ashtanga yoga are submission and acceptance of our own limitations.

But what if you aren't interested specifically in the Ashtanga lineage, or the sun god is just not for you? Could you still harness the religious power of yoga postures to affect what you believe or who you are?

I have no fidelity to the sun god, but a sun salutation nevertheless does instill in me a sense of humility and connection to something beyond myself. I personally associate corpse pose with gratitude, not death. For me, physical postures are opportunities to cultivate virtues, and the efficacy of my yoga is measured by my ability to foster specific character traits. This is another core portable idea from devotional yoga: Somatic practices can make you into a better version of yourself if you associate your core values with them.

Let me use another example, from the early days of COVID when we were frequently masking. I spent a lot of time talking to my then twelve-year-old daughter about why I thought it was important to wear a mask, because I knew physically masking every day would affect her. I told her our masks were to protect others, like our elderly neighbors, or Grandma and Grandpa. In this sense, wearing a mask was a way to cultivate compassion and kindness. If I had instead told her she needed to wear a mask for self-protection, wearing it might have cultivated selfishness and narcissism. The meanings we assign to our actions matter. They are part of what determines who we become.

The scholarly theory of virtue ethics is helpful for understanding how this works. Virtue ethics considers the cultivation of moral excellence to be important to living an ethical life. In many formulations, including in the work of Aristotle and Confucius, belief, understanding, and instruction are not enough to transform one into a good person. Specific actions—repetitive behavior and physical habits—are also part of moral development. A pianist's physical practice creates dexterity, muscle memory, and a good ear, all necessary to become a good musician. In the same way, religious practices transform the person who does them by creating dispositions to behave a certain way.

Virtue ethics teaches us that if we associate specific values with a physical asana practice, yoga can be part of a program of moral training. So when your yoga teacher asks you to set an intention at the beginning of class, do it! The only way for an asana practice to reinforce your core values is if you are intentional about it.

That brings me to the last advantage of restoring religion to yoga: It encourages us to think about yoga as a practice that can reinforce our connection and responsibility to others. Well-known yoga activist Susanna Barkataki argues that "we have incredible tools for calming the mind and body in yoga, but these tools were developed in a collectivist culture, not in the late-stage capitalist and individualist society we are in today." The idea that yoga is primarily a personal wellness technique is part of its American reinvention. And I'm not sure this can lead to real well-being. In fact, I think it might be getting in the way.

For instance, when a yoga teacher tells us to focus on good vibes and not sweat the small stuff, she is (unintentionally) giving us permission to ignore anything upsetting, including forms of injustice in the world. If we're using yoga only to "let everything go," we're missing part of its insight into well-being, namely that we have a responsibility to others. And understanding yoga's religious roots provides a way to think about it as inherently social.

Yogis like to remind us that the word *yoga* is derived from the Sanskrit root *yuj*, meaning "to unite," and Barkataki argues that the idea of unity isn't about skipping over forms of separation created by conflict, suffering, and violence. Part of the work toward unity is asking what prevents it. What are the systemic causes of our separation? And what can we do to change those? For Barkataki, the way to deepen your yoga practice is to embrace this broader view of unity, which she suggests requires several steps, including discovering how cultural appropriation drove yoga traditions underground and how power inequities influence the teaching and branding of modern yoga. Our first ladies of yoga are implicated in both these matters.

Devotional yoga also has resources for thinking about personal and social ethics more generally. If, when I mentioned linking your asana practice to your core values, you thought, *How do I know what my core values are?* yoga has some suggestions. One resource that several devotional yogic lineages offer comes from Patanjali's Yoga Sutra (c. 400 CE). When Patanjali describes yoga, he enumerates eight limbs. Postures or asanas are one limb, but as I mentioned earlier, another limb provides an ethical road map to right living: the yamas, roughly translated as "a set of restraints." Yamas offer five core principles to guide our actions. Ahimsa is practicing noninjury. Satya is truthfulness. Asteya is nonstealing. Brahmacharya is moderation. And finally, aparigraha, or nonattachment, letting go of what you do not need.

Consider how the yamas might help us think about our responsibility to others. Ahimsa, for instance, could urge us to consider whether the yoga businesses we support pay fair wages or have a commitment to diversity, inclusion, and accessibility. It not, we may inadvertently be contributing to the harm of others. A commitment to satya, or truthfulness, might prompt us to speak up about injustice or listen when others do. Asteya, or nonstealing, could help us (a) recognize how the U.S. yoga industry has benefited from the colonization of Indigenous and South Asian forms of knowledge, and (b) ask what sorts of reparations should be made.

Religious forms of yoga have built into them ways of thinking about a central role for ethics and well-being. When Devi, Folan, or the EUSD argue that yoga is a technique of self-care without this ethical content, they neglect a key resource that helps actualize real well-being.

2

Mind Cure

WHAT RELIGIOUS WORLDVIEWS AND MEDITATING MONKS CAN TEACH US ABOUT MINDFULNESS

Mindfulness—the mental technique of paying attention, being aware of the present moment, and reacting as little as possible—is undoubtedly the most widespread spiritual wellness practice in the United States. It is everywhere—hospitals, health clubs, colleges, corporations, military training facilities, and liberal churches. It can happen by sitting on a cushion with good posture, by attending to the breath or some other focal point, or merely by focusing the right way during mundane tasks. It is presented as the ultimate stress reducer and performance enhancer.

The university where I teach even has a mindfulness minor. When the applied psychology department reached out to me to collaborate on its development, I was skeptical. The minor didn't focus on the history of mindfulness or encourage critical thinking about how it's been used by corporations or the military. This was a minor that focused on life skills, framing meditation as a technique for career and mental health optimization. I didn't much like the idea of students thinking a watered-down religious practice could help their job performance.

Much as with the yoga controversy in Encinitas, no one was suggesting mindfulness exercises were religious—if they were, we certainly couldn't be offering them at our secular university—but everyone seemed aware their roots were in religion. (The very fact that the applied psychology department wanted religious studies faculty involved in the minor was an acknowledgment of this.) For mindfulness to be in our classrooms, we had to leave religious doctrines, metaphysics, and values behind. That seemed like the opposite of fostering religious literacy, which is my job as an educator.

Even the idea that mindfulness leads to good mental health outcomes for adolescents is problematic, since the randomized controlled trials of its effects on this age group are mixed. For instance, when the My Resilience in Adolescence (MYRIAD) project conducted studies of school-based mindfulness training on more than 28,000 children ages eleven to sixteen, they did not find the widespread benefits they'd predicted. Mindfulness didn't turn out to work any better "than usual social and emotional teaching in helping young people's mental health or well-being," they said. "It worked for some, but not for all." In part this is because adolescents aren't just mini adults; their metacognitive awareness and emotional self-regulation are less developed. They also already tend to be hyperfocused on their inner monologue, which means concentrating on their own thoughts can make them more, not less, anxious.

That brings me to my final concern about separating mindfulness from religion, namely that it assumes the practice is completely safe. How else could we justify offering it to adolescents in a nonclinical setting? But if mindfulness is powerful enough to affect our psychological health—if it is real medicine—wouldn't it also have side effects for some?

A phenomenon called *meditation sickness* or *adverse meditation effects* has been gaining more attention in the past decade, in part because of several high-profile cases of extreme forms of psychosis related to meditation. Hallucinations and dizziness, feelings of terror or depression, light sensitivity, excessive heat or coldness, and even suicides have all occurred after intensive meditation retreats or prolonged practice. One study found that more than 25 percent of meditators report adverse experiences.

Willoughby Britton, a psychologist at Brown University, has been studying the negative effects of meditation for several years and runs a clinic called Cheetah House. She frames meditation sickness as "too much of a good thing." For instance, although mindfulness training has helped patients with chronic pain through increased body awareness, body awareness can also be associated with depression, anxiety, and traumatic flashbacks. And while mindfulness has been shown to help with emotional regulation, Britton points to studies that have found it can also result in the "blunting, or complete loss of both positive and negative emotions and dissociation in some people." Similarly, some mindfulness meditation can help with sleep, but Britton and her colleagues found that once practice time begins to approach thirty minutes a day, sleep actually decreased as cortical arousal increased; as they put it, "awakening" turns out not to just be a metaphor! And yes, mindfulness can lead to acceptance of a particular situation a patient finds themselves in, but this is not a good thing if it prevents them from making changes that benefit them such as leaving a toxic relationship or a bad work environment.

My colleague Ira Helderman, who is a practicing psychotherapist, a religious studies scholar, and the author of *Prescribing the Dharma*, is currently working on a book about meditation sickness. He explained that although psychotherapists don't all agree on whether mindfulness is 100 percent secular, most categorize their work as nonreligious medical healing. And that is why he finds it so interesting that these same folks have turned to religious texts to try to understand the kinds of challenging meditation experiences they are hearing described by patients.

And this makes me wonder: Could mindfulness practice benefit in other ways from adding more of its religion back in?

Like so many other popular spiritual wellness practices, mindfulness has been watered down to make it universal, secular, and accessible to all. It is a quick, easy, cheap form of meditation that can be done anywhere at any time by anyone, earning it the name McMindfulness. This chapter is going to look a bit at the history of how that happened and consider what was left behind in the process. It will also describe my attempt to inject some religion back into mindfulness by attending a meditation retreat at a monastery—an experiment that had mixed results. Throughout, I want you to have a question in the back of your mind: Would a greater understanding of mindfulness's religious origins and context offer us a version of wellness that is more than managing our stress or increasing our productivity?

RELIGIOUS WORLDVIEWS

Let's start by introducing a concept from religious studies that will be helpful for understanding the relationship of mindfulness and religion: worldview. I first encountered this term reading the anthropologist Clifford Geertz while a doctoral student, but more recently I've come across it being used by psychiatrists trying to make sense of meditation sickness. Geertz famously described religions, and cultures, as having worldviews—models of reality. A religious worldview is a conception of the general order of existence that helps us make sense of the world around us, the nature of things, or the meaning of human life.

Worldviews are a big part of our well-being. They are the interpretive lens through which we understand our lives to have purpose and meaning. Worldviews inform what goals we should pursue, what experiences we find good or bad. They enable a shared understanding among individuals through a common frame of reference. By providing ways to interpret challenges when they arise, they help us respond, not just by providing theories but also by guiding behaviors. In other words, they help us ask ourselves both *Why did this happen?* and *What do I do now?*

Now let's think about mindfulness. Our worldview shapes the experience of mindfulness, affecting how we think about the purpose of mindfulness meditation as well as how we interpret its outcomes. But the techniques we use for mindfulness meditation were developed within specific religious worldviews. Ignoring that has consequences.

For instance, one way of thinking about meditation sickness is that it is the result of a worldview being called into question. When Helderman and I spoke on this issue, he pointed out that most of the psychological research on meditation sickness has been done on meditators of European descent who are living within Western worldviews. But mindfulness practices were originally developed in Asian and/or Buddhist worldviews. "Today you have people living in a very different context using these practices for very different purposes," he told me, "and

I've heard both psychotherapists and religious studies scholars suggest that it's *actually the resulting dissonance between worldviews* that is making these predominantly white meditators sick."

Say you approach meditation with a secular scientific worldview and interpret a mindfulness practice as aimed at something like self-improvement. But then you discover that the very technique you've been engaging in is based on the idea that the self is an illusion, so instead of improving yourself, you begin to call into question the very notion that you exist. Put differently, if you're engaging in a technique that assumes that the self is a fabrication but are hoping to gain a sense of control over the self, you're doomed to fail.

It's especially distressing to have an experience that puts into question our worldview because this undermines our coping mechanisms. We are left unmoored, with no way to make sense of what is happening to us. In that case, mindfulness meditation goes from being a technique for wellness to being a threat to well-being. If understanding the religious worldviews assumed by spiritual practices is part of how we can make them work better for us, it is also how we can be better informed about what we're getting ourselves into when we try out one of these practices.

MAINSTREAMING MINDFULNESS

Forms of contemplation are found in several religious traditions, but the version of mindfulness that went mainstream in the West is based on meditation techniques in early Buddhism. In his book *Rethinking Meditation*, Buddhist studies scholar David McMahan explains just how "unlikely" that was.

> *Consider for a moment how unlikely it is that practices developed by celibate recluses in South Asia over twenty-five centuries ago*

> *who renounced their possessions, homes, caste, and family identities to search their minds for a way to transcend sickness, ageing, and death—indeed the entire world—would be adapted to help middle-class professionals function better at work, bond with their families, manage their health, and find calm amid the frantic pace of modern life—even improve their golf game or sex life.*

This transformation depended on leaving the religious worldviews of mindfulness behind—something that often takes place when spiritual wellness practices are marketed to the masses. To get a sense of how it happened with mindfulness, let's go back and try to understand its roots.

We find references to *sati*, the Pali word that gets translated as "mindfulness," throughout the early Indian Buddhist canon, including the Satipatthana Sutta (circa 20 BCE). In this text, mindfulness is presented as a form of mental discipline for monks and described as "the direct path for the purification of beings, for the surmounting of sorrow and lamentation, for the disappearance of pain and grief, for the attainment of the true way."

Within the broader context of Buddhism, mindfulness is part of a group of mutually supporting practices known as the Noble Eightfold Path, which are:

1. Right understanding (*samma ditthi*)
2. Right thought (*samma sankappa*)
3. Right speech (*samma vaca*)
4. Right action (*samma kammanta*)
5. Right livelihood (*samma ajiva*)

6. Right effort (*samma vayama*)

7. Right mindfulness (*samma sati*)

8. Right concentration (*samma samadhi*)

Even if you know very little about Buddhism, you have likely heard of the Noble Eightfold Path. It is one of the Four Noble Truths in Buddhism: the path leading to the end of *dukkha,* or suffering. Sometimes called the Middle Way, because it helps us avoid the extremes of ascetism and overindulgence, the Noble Eightfold Path consists of practices that train us to see the world as it is and gain liberation or enlightenment. In other words, they are how we learn to interpret reality through a Buddhist worldview.

The Four Noble Truths

In Buddhism, the Four Noble Truths are:

1. The truth of suffering (dukkha)

2. The truth of the origin of suffering (samudāya)

3. The truth of the cessation of suffering (nirodha)

4. The truth of the path to the cessation of suffering (magga)

But as one of eight practices, why has mindfulness alone become synonymous with Buddhism in the West? Why was it promoted instead of others? And how did a technique only practiced by ordained monks and nuns prior to the twentieth century make its way into my secular university?

Buddhist Modernism

The story of how this happened begins with changes within Buddhism itself. One is the intellectual movement called Buddhist modernism, and another is the framing of meditation as a central Buddhist practice—which wasn't always the case.

Buddhism, more than any other major religion, has successfully rebranded itself as compatible with modern worldviews. This occurred through the contemporary movement that scholars refer to as Buddhist modernism.

Buddhist modernism interprets traditional Buddhist beliefs and practices in light of dominant modern cultural and intellectual forces like the Enlightenment, Protestantism, scientific rationalism, Romanticism, and psychology. It began under the conditions of colonialism in the nineteenth century, but don't think of it as simply "Western Buddhism." Asian Buddhists also used Buddhist modernism to protect their practice from external threats, and they have been key agents in its global transmission. It is more accurate to say that Buddhist modernism is the result of the interaction of the West and Asia over the last 150 years.

One early iteration of Buddhist modernism occurred in the mid-nineteenth century, when Western scholars such as the Welsh Orientalist Thomas W. Rhys Davids began to insist the "true Buddhism" was found in ancient texts. This is a narrow and rather Protestant way of thinking about religion; in addition to *sola fide* (discussed in the last chapter), many branches of Protestantism also emphasize the doctrine of *sola scriptura*, which states that the Bible is the only true authority on Christianity, rather than ancient traditions, clerical decrees, and so on. This textual bias was internalized by Western scholars who studied Buddhism. Most assumed that texts would be the best authority in that tradition as well, and this approach made it easier for them to focus on aspects of Buddhism compatible with modern Western sensibilities and ignore common Buddhist practices that were not—things like karmic metaphysics, spirit worship, fortune-telling, and monastic life.

And then there was the question of which texts became seen as canonical, since Buddhism didn't have the equivalent of a single, widely accepted Bible. For instance, Davids focused exclusively on Buddhist texts that discussed ethics and philosophy rather than those that discussed supernatural events, hell realms, or rebirth. This allowed him to insist that the Buddha's original message was a rational, psychological, and ethical philosophy.

Buddhist reformers made similar interpretative moves for strategic reasons. For instance, when British colonists portrayed Asian Buddhist communities as superstitious, passive, and nihilistic in order to justify "saving" the locals with Christianity, Buddhists defended their tradition in ways that were legible to Westerners. They presented Buddhism as rational, active, ethical, and most importantly, compatible with modern scientific knowledge. This last idea—that Buddhism is scientific—proved to be an enduring core idea of Buddhist modernism and became key to arguments that mindfulness was appropriate in secular institutions like hospitals, corporations, and schools.

Monastic Meditation Revival

Before we can get to how mindfulness went mainstream, we must understand another change that happened in Buddhism: the elevation of meditation to a central practice.

Now, you may think all Buddhists meditate. And yes, meditation is an important practice for Buddhists today, especially those in the West. But that was not always the case. In fact, quite the opposite. Even if the *theory* of meditation was traditionally taught to ordained monks and nuns, before the nineteenth century, it wasn't consistently *practiced*. In fact, in Theravada Buddhist meditation—the form most associated with mainstream mindfulness today—the practice almost died out entirely by the tenth century. It wasn't until the rise of Buddhist modernism that meditation, particularly the form known as *vipassana*, was promoted as another way to protect Buddhism from outside threats.

In his book *The Birth of Insight*, Erik Braun identifies the Burmese monk Ledi Sayadaw (1846–1923) as the founder of mass vipassana meditation. Ledi believed that under British occupation, the best way to ensure the survival of Buddhism in Burma (now known as Myanmar) was to spread and strengthen the practice of Buddhism among the laity as well as the monastics. As a result, he encouraged ordinary Buddhists to engage in practices usually reserved for monks and nuns. That included studying canonical texts like the Abhidhamma, which provides an in-depth exploration of the Buddha's teachings and the practice of vipassana meditation.

According to Braun, vipassana, or insight meditation, is "the mindful observation (*sati*) of reality that confirms the lessons of Buddhism at a transformative level." The goal is to gain insight, to see things as they really are. Traditionally, a monastic would master *samatha,* or calming meditation, before attempting vipassana. To make it accessible to a wide range of Buddhists, however, Ledi said it was fine to practice vipassana without proficiency in other forms of concentration.

The mass meditation movement came west in the twentieth century when some very prominent South Asian monks—teachers like Thich Nhat Hanh and Bhante Henepola Gunaratana—began to teach meditation techniques to Western lay Buddhists and non-Buddhists alike. Rebranding them as mindfulness, they drew on several meditative Buddhist traditions for training the mind. Their pitch was clear: Buddhist meditation was consistent with the modern psychological understanding of the human and an example of how Buddhism was valuable to modern life.

Let's look a little closer at Bhante Henepola Gunaratana's own "discovery" of mindful meditation. Bhante G, as he is known by his followers, was born in rural Sri Lanka in 1927 and ordained at the age of twenty. He was an early adopter of mindfulness meditation, but not exactly by choice. He tells the story of how this happened in his autobiography, *Journey to Mindfulness.*

Shortly after becoming a full Theravada monk in 1947, Bhante G participated in a ritual, known as *paritta,* to drive away evil spirits. This is an intense ritual, in which pairs of monks tag-team each other in order to chant loudly and continuously for seven days. Bhante G explains that usually monks only take one shift for the week, but as young and ambitious newly ordained monks, he and his chanting partner convinced some older monks to give them their turns. As he tells it, he ended up chanting almost nonstop for the entire week, pausing only to eat and use the bathroom. By the end of the week, he was "in bad shape" and "suffering some kind of nervous breakdown." He went from being a star pupil with a photographic memory to failing his final exams because he was unable to recognize any alphabet or to read. He suddenly had severe headaches, temper problems, and insomnia.

His community's Buddhist worldview included the belief that spirits affect our world—the entire reason for the paritta was to drive away evil spirits. Thus, the simplest explanation for what had happened to Bhante G was that he had become possessed by some evil spirit. His teacher arranged for eight monks to conduct a night-long chanting session over him. No improvement. His parents called in an exorcist. That didn't work either. His teacher gave him a talisman made of copper to wear around his neck. Nothing. At the time, these were all common Buddhist treatments for this sort of affliction, but none of them were effective.

Then Bhante G had an idea. He thought maybe meditation could help. "When my friends heard that plan, they burst out laughing," he writes. That was because in the 1940s, the practice of meditation was hardly common for monks: "Although I was well-versed in the theory of meditation . . . I had never actually meditated, believe it or not. Very few monks did in those days. They were too busy preaching Dhamma [dharma], chanting, and performing blessing ceremonies." Bhante G had even heard meditation could cause mental disturbance. As Jeff Wilson, the author of *Mindful America*, puts it, at that time, "to engage in mindfulness in order to heal oneself was literally the act of a madman."

Bhante G figured that since he was already disturbed, he had nothing to lose. He secretly began to meditate whenever he could. And it worked! He was able to read again, and his memory and temper improved.

This began a journey that would make Bhante G one of the most influential mindfulness advocates in the West. In 1968, he moved to the United States and taught what was becoming known as mindfulness in several settings in the Washington, DC, area, including at the Washington Buddhist Vihara and as the Buddhist chaplain at American University. In 1985, he founded the Bhavana Society in rural West Virginia to teach free vipassana meditation retreats. His 1992 book, *Mindfulness in Plain English,* was published in the midst of an explosion of interest in mindfulness, and became a standard meditation manual for American Buddhists.

Bhante G is an example of a Buddhist who promoted mindfulness for non-Buddhists. But there are also important mindfulness advocates who position themselves outside of Buddhist communities. They present mindfulness as evidence-based medical therapy and insist we can engage in mindfulness without ever having to dabble in Buddhism. One of the best-known advocates in this group is Jon Kabat-Zinn.

Medicalizing Mindfulness

Kabat-Zinn was introduced to Buddhism while working toward his PhD in molecular biology at MIT in the late 1960s. He was immediately hooked. He went on to study with Buddhist teachers like Thich Nhat Hanh and Korean Zen master Seung Sahn. He was involved in early meditation centers in the United States, trained and taught at Insight Meditation Society, was an active member of the Mind & Life Institute, and helped found the Cambridge Zen Center in 1973. His greatest contribution to the mindfulness movement, however, was developing the mindfulness-based stress reduction (MBSR) program that would bring mindfulness to thousands by embedding it in secular spaces like hospitals, corporations, and universities.

The idea for MBSR came to Kabat-Zinn during a two-week vipassana retreat at the Insight Meditation Society. While participating in an intensive meditation workshop he had a vision, which he describes as his "karmic assignment," to bring Buddhist meditation to mainstream Western medical culture by adapting the practice to the specific needs and interests of patients.

As a result, he created the mindfulness-based stress reduction (MBSR) program. The program combines in-clinic sitting and walking meditations with audio-guided home assignments to treat stress and pain. It emphasizes tools for approaching everyday activities, like eating, with mindful intention. Today, more than thirty thousand people have completed the course, which is offered in every state and in more than 720 medical centers and clinics nationwide and abroad. Other new therapies have also adopted Buddhist mindfulness meditation within the worldview of Western medicine, among them dialectical behavior therapy (DBT), acceptance and commitment therapy (ACT), and mindfulness-based interventions (MBIs), focusing on topics like addiction, parenting, eating, art, and relationships.

Kabat-Zinn said famously in 2006 that "mindfulness is the heart of Buddhist practice, but it has nothing to do with Buddhism." He thought extracting mindfulness from Buddhist religious worldviews was necessary to presenting it as a legitimate treatment for mainstream medical care. And he had a couple of tactics for doing so.

First, Kabat-Zinn leaned into who he was—and who he wasn't. As a white, non-Buddhist PhD overseeing a university-sponsored clinic, Kabat-Zinn had the academic and scientific authority to present mindfulness as acceptable and safe to Western audiences. Compare this to Maharishi Mahesh Yogi, the bearded Indian founder of Transcendental Meditation (TM), a form of meditation that gained followers in the 1960s and '70s but failed to gain the widespread acceptance of MBSR. As Wilson writes, "Reaction to TM was often mediated by stereotypes of 'Oriental monks' applied to the Maharishi, the iconic face of the movement. Jon Kabat-Zinn, the face of MBSR, is a clean-shaven white American doctor with short hair and rimless glasses, who delivered his teachings in business attire."

Second, Kabat-Zinn leveraged a psychological interpretation of Buddhism. As we have seen, early Western scholars of Buddhism, such as Rhys Davids, focused on textual discussions of the mind and human cognition. Asian Buddhist modernist popularizers, such as the Japanese Zen teacher D. T. Suzuki, likewise presented Buddhism as containing psychological truths. By the mid-twentieth century, Buddhist meditation was commonly interpreted therapeutically as a way to heal from destructive habits and repressed memories. And for Kabat-Zinn, the safe way to talk about the essence of mindfulness was to say it was a psychological, evidence-based treatment.

Third, he erased some Buddhist elements and redefined others. For instance, he didn't integrate references to Buddhist gods, enlightenment, and reincarnation—elements of Buddhism that weren't scientifically testable—into MBSR. But he took this a step further and translated some Buddhist terminology into more scientific-sounding terms. *Dharma*, for example, is a Sanskrit word that refers to the Buddha's teachings. Kabat-Zinn redefined dharma as "law" to separate the term from Buddhism. He performed a similar sleight of hand with *karma*, defining it with terms more often associated with physics than with religion. "Karma means that this happens because that happened," he writes. "B is connected to A, every effect has an antecedent cause, and every cause an effect that is its measure and its consequence, at least at the non-quantum level." By claiming karma was a system of cause and effect—not a fixed destiny—Kabat-Zinn could also argue it was universal and thus could not be owned exclusively by Buddhists.

Finally, Kabat-Zinn legitimized these adjustments of Buddhism with the Buddhist concept *upaya-kausalya*, or "skillful means." Traditionally associated with the Mahayana branch, skillful means is the adaptation of Buddhism to best reach and serve a specific audience. When the Buddha or advanced bodhisattvas, for whom skillful means was traditionally reserved, invoke this concept, they are understood to be doing so with wisdom and compassion for those who are "farther back on the path." In order to bring mindfulness meditation practices to the masses, Kabat-Zinn essentially deputized himself to use skillful means. In other words, the success of MBSR was based on Kabat-Zinn's intentional extraction of mindfulness from a religious worldview, which, ironically, he justified with a concept from that worldview.

The more I learned about Kabat-Zinn, the more I wondered what was lost when he jettisoned so much of the religious content and context of mindfulness. To try to figure this out, I headed to Bhante G's West Virginia monastery for a week-long silent vipassana meditation retreat—the type of retreat that inspired Jon Kabat-Zinn to create MBSR in the first place.

MONASTIC MINDFULNESS AT BHAVANA SOCIETY

Seeing my suitcase by the front door, my daughter asked where I was going for research this week. I told her I was headed to a silent retreat at Bhavana Society, a monastery in rural West Virginia, to learn more about Buddhist meditation.

"That doesn't seem like much fun," she said.

I sort of felt the same.

Don't get me wrong. I was excited to interview the Sri Lankan monks at Bhavana—especially Bhante G, who had played such an important role in popularizing mindfulness in the West. And I did think attending a vipassana-style meditation workshop was a good way to learn about the missing role of religion in mainstream mindfulness. But sitting meditation is really challenging for me. Not the silence part, not the concentration part—the sitting part. My suitcase had a bottle of Advil and a foam roller.

Bhavana Society is more than two hours from the nearest airport. That meant a very expensive taxi ride. My Ethiopian driver and I chatted the whole way, and when we finally reached the monastery, it was so remote—a good thirty minutes from the nearest town—I could tell he didn't want to leave me there.

"No, it's okay. I'm here to study this community," I said, thinking maybe that would explain my interest in this off-the-grid location.

"But who are these people?" he asked, side-eying the tall monk with a shaved head in orange robes walking toward us.

He was visibly startled when the monk leaned in through the open passenger's-side window and said, "Thank you for bringing her," and then, "What is your name?"

"Kareem," he replied.

"I hope I will see you again, Kareem," the monk answered.

Poor Kareem couldn't get out of there fast enough.

Even if my cabdriver wasn't interested in monastic life, a taste of it was exactly what I was hoping for. And I quickly discovered the retreat was designed to do just that.

For instance, we were required to follow the eight monastic precepts—rules for right moral behavior that help cultivate virtue, namely abstaining from killing, stealing, lying, sexual activity, intoxicants, eating at the wrong time, self-adornments like cosmetics, and sleeping on luxurious beds.

The Eight Precepts

The eight Buddhist monastic precepts are:

1. I undertake the precept to refrain from destroying living creatures.

2. I undertake the precept to refrain from taking that which is not given.

3. I undertake the precept to refrain from sexual activity.

4. I undertake the precept to refrain from incorrect speech.

5. I undertake the precept to refrain from intoxicating drinks and drugs which lead to carelessness.

6. I undertake the precept to refrain from eating at the forbidden time (i.e., after noon).

7. I undertake the precept to refrain from dancing, singing, music, going to see entertainments, wearing garlands, using perfumes, and beautifying the body with cosmetics.

8. I undertake the precept to refrain from lying on a high or luxurious sleeping place.

To encourage us to remain celibate for the duration of the retreat (precept 3), men and women slept in single-sex dorms or rustic wooden cabins. I was placed alone in a small unheated cabin with no electricity. It was definitely not a luxurious sleeping place (precept 8). We had two communal meals a day, breakfast and lunch, and no food after noon (precept 6). ("We find that because a meditation retreat isn't physically rigorous, most people can get by with two high-quality meals a day," Bhavana's website explains. "Not eating late in the day tends to make people less drowsy" and "it also frees up more time for practice.") Cell phone use was prohibited, as was watching movies or television shows in our free time (precept 7). That was helped by the fact that there was no cell signal on most of the grounds and no internet access in any of the sleeping quarters. And we took a vow of silence for the entirely of our stay. That prevented us from incorrect speech (precept 4), like lying.

The retreat schedule was quite rigorous. Our first meditation started at 5:30 a.m., and the last one ended around 8:00 p.m. This meant that for most of the five days, I was sitting on a cushion on the floor of the meditation hall. As expected, that was quite painful for my back and hips. But my physical discomfort had a payoff, because I did get some insight into a form of mindfulness that explicitly embraced a Buddhist worldview, particularly during the dharma talks. And here are some of my big takeaways.

For one thing, mindfulness was presented as more than therapeutic. Bhante Ethkandawaka Saddhajeewa, or Bhante S, is the co-abbot of the Bhavana Society. He explained in his first dharma talk that "mindfulness for the wrong goals, like destressing or achievement, is not Buddhist." Instead, he urged us to think about mindfulness as a way to cleanse ourselves—and, he joked, "We need a lot of detergent!" But it is not to be instrumentalized for specific goals. In fact, part of practicing real mindfulness, he explained, is being detached from specific outcomes. We don't know what will happen after we improve our awareness and concentration, Bhante S said. All we do know is that what comes next "won't happen overnight."

A second theme of the retreat was that real mindfulness should be combined with other practices, like observing the eight monastic precepts. Otherwise it was "dangerous." Bhante S repeated over and over that meditation was only one leg of a three-legged stool. I learned later from my colleague and Buddhism scholar Nalika Gajaweera that he was referencing the conceptual trilogy of *dana sila bhavana*. Gajaweera explained to me that this theory, which comes from the Theravada tradition, describes three sorts of good actions: generous ones (dana), moral ones (sila), and ones that develop our mental capacities (bhavana). Mindful meditation is an example of bhavana, but it is only one leg of the stool. Following the precepts is an example of sila. There are also right actions directed toward others, or dana.

Gajaweera (who told me, "Dana is my jam!") gave me two examples of dana: philanthropy and patronage. For the first example, she pointed me to a brief piece she wrote about the Sri Lankan Buddhist philanthropist Kushil Gunasekera. Kushil's philanthropy is inspired by a Buddhist worldview that sees generosity as a kind of spiritual vocation based on karma, rebirth, and spiritual merit. As Gajaweera describes it, generosity is part of becoming "a karmically moral subject." Or as Kushil puts it, "The more you give, the more will be yours to give."

Giving donations to monks and Buddhist institutions, such as the Bhavana Society, is also an example of how to cultivate an ethic of generosity, or dana. So, if we were properly following the entire conceptual trilogy of dana sila bhavana, we would be leaving a check in the donation box before leaving the retreat.

But it is likely that most American retreat participants skipped this, because Gajaweera has found in her research that dana is much more common within Sri Lankan Buddhist communities. In her research among Western Buddhists, Gajaweera has consistently noted a reluctance to take teaching about karma, rebirth, and spiritual merit—concepts that help explain why dana is important to a good life—seriously. She concludes, "Indeed, many Buddhist converts dismiss these more orthodox teachings as cultural accretions that have little apparent relevance to twenty-first-century lives."

What makes sila/precepts and dana/generosity curiously understressed in the West, when the third leg of the stool, mindfulness/bhavana, is so popular? One way to understand this is as evidence of competing worldviews. When U.S.-based Buddhist converts privilege scientific worldviews—so dominant in our cultural context—they are more likely to reject the ideas about good karmic merit and happy rebirth that ground dana. Likewise, for people whose philosophical worldviews are based on liberalism, following precepts feels like a constraint to their individual freedom. It makes sense that the particulars of a Buddhist worldview that challenge dominant Western ones would be missing from mainstream Western mindfulness.

I also learned quite a bit about Buddhist mindfulness from one-on-one conversations with the monks. On day three, I even had a private conversation with Bhante G. He was a week away from his ninety-seventh birthday, making him not only one of the most senior monks on the planet but also one of the oldest. He spends most of his day alone in his quarters, emerging only for mealtimes and to deliver a daily dharma talk, which the Bhavana Society streams for free on their website. But during our retreat, he agreed to meet with me privately.

Bhante G's voice was a bit weak, but I found him to be sharp and engaging. I asked him for stories to share with my students, to help get them beyond thinking of mindfulness as a quick and easy fix. He seemed pleased with this request and gave me three gems, each with their own lesson.

He began by asking, "You know the story about Tortoise and Hare, but do you know the story about the second time they raced?" I shook my head and got my pen ready. For their second race, Bhante G told me, Hare proposed a new course that involved crossing a river. His reasoning was simple. He thought, *I can just jump over the river, while Tortoise will be stuck on this side.* So Tortoise set off, and Hare rested, took it easy. But Hare had forgotten that Tortoise was amphibious. When Tortoise reached the river, he slid easily down the bank, swam across, and climbed back out. Despite Hare's plan to cheat, Tortoise won again. "There is no cheating in real mindfulness," Bhante G said.

"There is no cheating in real mindfulness."

In the next story, he introduced me to Snail, who lived in a lush green garden under an enormous frangipani tree that would bloom every spring. Those pink flowers looked tasty to Snail, but the size of the tree and his speed made climbing to the top seem an impossible feat. Nevertheless, one fall day, Snail decided to give it a try, and he began to climb the enormous tree. A group of children playing nearby asked him what he was doing. When he said he wanted to eat the flowers at the top of the tree, the children laughed at him and said, "There are only leaves up there! You're wasting your time." Snail responded, "By the time I get there, there will be flowers." And he continued climbing. He moved slowly, day by day, week by week. It wasn't easy going, but Snail persevered. By spring, he reached the top of the tree and found it full of pink blossoms. "You need to believe that your hard work will have results," Bhante G told me, "even if you can't see what those will be right now."

But my favorite story, the one I've shared the most since I heard it, helps explain why picking and choosing from the spiritual salad bar might not be working for us. "If you come to me asking how to find water," he said, "I will tell you to drill a hundred-foot hole. But if you then try to dig ten holes of ten feet each, you will be wasting your time." I smiled at that and nodded in agreement. "You confuse your practice if you do too many practices," he continued. "If you change too quickly, without perfecting one, you will never progress. Pick one spot and drill."

On day four, I had a private conversation with the other senior monk, Bhante S. I started by asking the difference between monastic mindfulness and what he was teaching us. He replied that, as a monk, he was on the expressway to enlightenment, and that it was important to remember that most people were in the slow lane. Ordinary meditators may have the same goal, but we shouldn't expect to get there quickly. Adopting a religious practice as an outsider isn't a shortcut.

Bhante S and I bonded a bit about being teachers when he told me about his early days in the classroom, but he also confessed how wonderful it was now to be removed from that sort of exhausting work. He appreciated being way out in rural West Virginia, where, in his words, "people don't bother me." He could focus his time and energy on pursuing enlightenment.

My takeaway from that part of the conversation was probably much different than Bhante S intended. "Enlightenment will blow up your life," he told me. I wasn't sure I wanted the sort of transformation his version of real mindfulness offered. At least not in the way he meant. My life is full of others "bothering me," whether my students, colleagues, friends, or family. To meet those social obligations requires energy on my part, sure, but it also gives my life meaning. Withdrawal from the world—and avoidance of political action or service to others—wasn't consistent with what I thought real well-being would look like, at least not for me.

If I'm being honest, I left my monastery retreat a bit unsatisfied. Something was still missing for me. Part of this was likely the limitations of the workshop model. In their contribution to the volume *What's Wrong with Mindfulness (and What Isn't)*, Barry Magid and Marc Poirier explain why a retreat or workshop might not be the best way to learn about Buddhist mindfulness meditation:

> *Instead of the deep, repetitive ongoing immersion in a complex ritual form that gradually, sometimes only over the course of many years, reveals itself, the workshop goer instead is offered a smorgasbord of chants, texts, and practices that offer the aura of the exotic or of a deracinated mysticism, but without the opportunity to actually engage a single coherent traditional form in any depth.*

That was how I felt: like I had barely scratched the surface. Or as Bhante G might put it, I felt like I hadn't even learned enough to start to dig a hole. You can't really learn a practice, or the worldview that gives it meaning and efficacy, in a few days.

RESTORING RELIGION TO MINDFULNESS

Mindful meditation techniques are not neutral ways to train our minds. They were developed within a religious worldview and are, as Buddhist studies scholar Jared Lindahl puts it, "methods for cultivating specific experiences and for contemplating experience in accordance with Buddhist norms and doctrines."

Even mindfulness practices that people try to call "secular" are not value-free, and they can conflict with the commitments folks already have. Ira Helderman gave me a good example of this. He said that while Kabat-Zinn would say the practice of observing your thoughts nonjudgmentally can benefit everyone, "a Catholic that believes one can have sinful thoughts that need to be confessed could have a real problem with that." For those of us who do not identify as Buddhist, that means mindfulness will likely "work better for us" if we find versions of these practices that line up with our own worldviews and core values.

In my opinion, the lack of alignment between the medical and monastic versions of mindfulness is unsatisfactory. For me, Kabat-Zin's MBSR gave up too much of the Buddhist worldview. But my time at Bhavana Society made it clear that returning to a monastic form of mindfulness wasn't compatible with my life. In some ways, after months of research, I was back to the drawing board, trying to find a version of mindfulness that was both more Buddhist and more responsive to the demands of modern life.

By framing the challenge in this way, I finally realized what was missing for me from both the versions of mindfulness I'd been exploring: social engagement. In her book *American Dharma*, religious studies scholar Ann Gleig describes how some American Buddhist communities have come to this realization as well. "Whereas members of the first generation of American convert teachers have focused on using Buddhism to address individual psychological suffering," she explains, "Buddhist principles are now being applied to the sociocultural dimensions of that individual self and the collective suffering."

When I started looking for a more socially engaged mindfulness, things started to finally click. In *American Dharma*, for instance, Gleig describes how mindfulness is used to tackle racism. This work begins by seeing racism as a form of suffering, or dukkha, as defined in the first Noble Truth. Next, there is an inquiry into what causes this specific suffering. Within a Buddhist worldview, racism can be seen as the result of the existential tendency to create a false sense of self and an unreal other whom we fear or hate. It is the cultural manifestation of the illusion of separateness. Mindfulness practice, in this context, can help to free us from this cultural conditioning. Eleanor Hancock, who developed the White Awake training for the Insight Meditation Community of Washington, says, "Doing racial awareness work is part of reclaiming our full humanity." And that is a goal that goes much deeper than wellness.

Another way to make mindfulness more socially engaged is by restoring the central role of the *sangha*, a community of shared practice. A sangha is one of the Three Jewels of Buddhism, alongside the Buddha (the teacher) and the dharma (the teachings). It plays a crucial role in preserving and transmitting the teachings of the Buddha, providing support for practice, and fostering a sense of community. Larry Yang, cofounder of the East Bay Meditation Center in Oakland, California, and author of *Awakening Together*, believes a robust sangha is necessary for helping us understand the real purpose of mindfulness: "The practice is not just about our own personal awakening, enlightenment, or freedom. The path is not just about personal salvation. It is about our collective journey and transformation toward a shared experience of wisdom and tenderness."

Practicing mindfulness within a sangha of like-minded people has the potential to make it more meaningful and effective. For instance, in her studies of sanghas specifically for people of color, Gajaweera has found they create a safe space in which

"PoC meditators move from experiencing painful emotions as individual experience to understanding them as collective experiences shaped by socio-political conditions and shared by other racialized minorities." This, she finds, "fosters a type of resilience."

Therapeutic use of mindfulness might be headed in the engaged mindfulness direction as well. "Since the invention of talk therapy," Helderman points out, "clinicians have debated whether psychotherapy should, indeed, seek to do more than only cure psychological illnesses." In fact, Helderman writes, "some therapists consider Buddhist traditions to be the ultimate antidote to psychotherapies they see as overly focused on the isolated individual." To that end, therapists have more recently started proposing what they call "second generation mindfulness-based interventions" that are intentionally embedded in Buddhist worldviews and a larger Buddhist ethical context that would foster social engagement. They hold up Buddhist teachings on the interrelatedness of all human beings "as a crucial corrective that should revise existing psychological theories."

I see these engaged forms of mindfulness, which draw purpose and values from a religious worldview like Buddhism or other collective visions of the world, as something that can do more than make us healthier and happier. I see them as potentially helping us transform our current context into a more livable world. The portable idea here is that having clarity about the purpose of mindful meditation is important, as is making sure that purpose is consistent with who you are and who you want to be. What is the purpose you are working toward, and might it be more complex than reducing your cortisol levels?

And what about a university's mindfulness minor? Are there lessons here for how it could be salvaged?

While I did consider trying to fight the existence of the minor entirely, in the end, I decided instead to try to influence it to be more conducive to engaged mindfulness. First, I insisted the minor require one religious studies course focused on Asian religious traditions. This ensures students learn at least something about the religious worldviews that mindfulness meditation comes from.

My second condition was to require a course for the minor that would problematize the very idea of it. A course that explains how colonialism and Protestantism played a role in promoting mindfulness, highlights the erasure involved in medicalized mindfulness, asks if mindfulness is as effective and safe as we have been told, and explores what mindfulness connected to a religious worldview would look like. A course that asks, *Would a more engaged form of mindfulness help us achieve well-being beyond individual self-optimization?* A course, in short, that would do much of the work in this chapter.

I teach this course. Its official title in the course catalogue is Selling Spirituality, but I tell students the first day of class that it is the Mindfulness Killjoy course. Its purpose it to unsettle all their assumptions about what mindfulness is and what it is not. And make them question the purpose of mindfulness in the first place.

3

Higher Power

ALCOHOLICS ANONYMOUS'S GOD-TALK LESSONS FOR THE ADDICT IN ALL OF US

Whatever obstacles I personally face to living a flourishing and fully human life, addiction to drugs and alcohol is not one of them. I ate some pot brownies by mistake in college when my boyfriend's roommate left them in their fridge and hated the experience of being high. I wouldn't take the OxyContin my doctor prescribed in my thirties for my back pain. I allow myself only one annual refill of my prescription of Ambien to help deal with jet lag. I don't drink at all.

The reason I abstain from alcohol is not some vague commitment to health. I don't drink because my father drank too much. One of my earliest memories is sneaking a sip of my dad's screwdriver as a three-year-old; I dislike orange juice to this day. I didn't see him drunk—at least what registered to me as drunk—until I was in my forties, but I always knew he was an alcoholic and for that reason have avoided alcohol most of my adult life.

My father's drinking contributed to my parents' divorce during my senior year of high school. When we had a family intervention for him when he was seventy, it was because my stepmother confessed he had been passing out during the day and hiding bottles around the house. That intervention ended with him getting into a car and driving directly to a Betty Ford clinic to begin a thirty-day residential program. It was there he experienced Alcoholics Anonymous (AA) for the first time.

But AA never worked for him. He told me he found the program "too religious" and only quit drinking for good when he was diagnosed with what proved to be fatal pancreatic cancer.

Given that I don't struggle with addiction and AA didn't work for my dad, you might be wondering why I included a chapter on this topic. AA is not really associated with the "wellness industry" in the same way as yoga or mindfulness meditation. Gwyneth Paltrow is not trying to sell me a twelve-step program bundled with a jade vagina egg. And yet AA *is* aimed at getting healthier and happier. AA's founders and participants *do* insist spirituality is the key to successfully working the program. And AA is also credited with popularizing the phrase "spiritual but not religious." The prevalence of mindfulness notwithstanding, AA is probably the most widely accepted form of spirituality as a therapeutic technique.

Despite its founders and members insisting it is not religious, and despite the diverse religious commitments of its early members, there is no way around the fact that AA has explicitly religious roots. It initially came out of the Oxford Group, a Protestant organization, and its twelve steps are an expansion of the Oxford Group's six steps for avoiding sin. Much of the rhetorical language in its foundational literature—*The Big Book* and *Twelve Steps and Twelve Traditions*—is also Christian. Submitting to a higher power is step two of the program, and God is mentioned in an additional five of the twelve steps. References to God are common in meetings, many of which conclude with the Serenity Prayer: "God grant me the serenity to accept the things I cannot change, the courage to change the things I can, and the wisdom to know the difference."

The religious roots of AA have caused problems for more people than just my dad, including those concerned about the role of AA programs in drug sentencing and prison rehabilitation. The *Griffin v. Coughlin* cases are a good example. In the 1990s, David Griffin, an inmate at Shawangunk Correctional Facility in New York, was approved for a special extended visitation program as a reward for his good behavior. But there was a catch. Since Griffin had a history of heroin use, participation in the Alcohol and Substance Abuse Treatment Program (ASAT) was a condition of these new visitation privileges. The ASAT entailed 330 hours of therapy made up of lectures, seminars, group discussions, and counseling, 26 hours of which were Alcoholic Anonymous meetings.

Griffin, a self-described atheist, participated in the ASAT program for a couple of months and then filed a grievance. The program was just too religious for him. In his complaint, he argued that integrating AA's Twelve Steps into a state-sponsored substance abuse program was an unconstitutional establishment of religion. His initial grievance was denied, and he filed a suit with the Supreme Court of New York, which rejected his claim without an evidentiary hearing, as did the Appellate Division. But in 1996, the New York Court of Appeals found the Twelve Steps of AA did amount to religion, and that "adherence to the AA fellowship entails engagement in religious activity and religious proselytization."

On one hand, Griffin and the New York Court of Appeals

are correct. Despite how the program and participants internally describe the program, mainly as "spiritual but not religious," it is reasonable to conclude that AA is religious—in origin, in content, in the rhetoric of its texts, and in what you hear in a group meeting.

On the other hand, I don't think the ASAT program violates the Establishment Clause of the First Amendment. Yes, it exposed Griffin to theological ideas—those of AA's founders and those of his fellow inmates—and urged him to adopt some of his own. But the program didn't dictate what those religious ideas would be. Bill Wilson, one of the cofounders of AA, was clear: "Alcoholics Anonymous does not demand that you believe anything." But it does suggest you believe *something.* It doesn't endorse one religion, but it is also not irreligious.

The point of this chapter is to explain what the popularity of AA—and the fact that it seems to work for so many—can teach us about well-being. Yes, AA is a specific therapy to deal with a specific problem. But AA's God talk has insights even those of us who aren't actively working toward sobriety can learn from. And this chapter will explain why.

BILL WILSON'S GOD PROBLEM

The telling of the history of AA often starts in 1935 in Akron, Ohio, when by happenstance Bill Wilson and Dr. Bob Smith—who those in the program refer to as simply Bill W and Dr. Bob—discovered together how one drunk can help another toward sobriety. But Bill's sobriety didn't begin with his friendship with Dr. Bob in the summer of 1935. It began with a visit from his old school friend Ebby Thacher.

If Bill W was a drunk, it was common knowledge that his friend Ebby was even worse. Ebby had even been committed to an insane asylum for drunkenness, something Bill had managed to avoid. But in the fall of 1934, Ebby, sober for two months, paid a visit to Bill, who was drunk as a skunk on gin. How had Ebby managed to find a cure when Bill had not?

According to Bill's version of that encounter, Ebby shared with him that his sobriety began when he joined the Oxford Group, which was founded by American Lutheran minister Frank Buchman in 1921 as a way to follow Jesus's basic commandments without the baggage of institutional Christianity. No formal membership, no church, no clergy—a loose, unchurched Christian fellowship, if you like. And it was through the Oxford Group that Ebby said he "got religion." Bill wasn't initially impressed by this revelation. "Last summer an alcoholic crackpot; now, I suspected, a little cracked about religion," he wrote while recounting the meeting.

As is clear from that comment, Bill W was no fan of religion. He distrusted organized religion, which he believed was a negative force in the world. He was not an atheist, because, in his words, that required too much certainty, but he was an agnostic for sure. He certainly didn't think religion would be part of his own rehabilitation. But given Ebby's miraculous recovery, he was intrigued. Was religion really the key to Ebby's sobriety? If so, could it work for him?

Ebby suggested Bill attend some Oxford Group meetings to find out. Bill hemmed and hawed, stating his lack of belief in God made it a bad fit for him. But Ebby had a solution: "Why don't you choose your own conception of God?" And this suggestion was just the sort of opening Bill needed.

For two years, Bill leaned in hard on the Oxford Group. He regularly attended their meetings, "witnessed" his personal spiritual experiences, and tried to abide by their six principles for combating sin: performing self-inventory, admitting wrongs, making amends, using prayer and meditation, and carrying the message to others. And it seemed to work. Bill W got sober.

Even when Bill left the group to found AA with Dr. Bob, he retained much of what he had learned about religion. He used the Oxford Group's six principles as the basis of AA's Twelve Steps. He retained a central role for fellowship. He insisted members had to accept a higher power. He made having a "spiritual experience" key to the alcoholic's sobriety. Bill W had become a believer that religion was the key to sobriety. He just didn't want to call it that.

The God Problem in AA's Twelve Steps

Here are the Twelve Steps of AA, with references to God in bold:

1. We admitted we were powerless over alcohol—that our lives had become unmanageable.

2. Came to believe **that a Power greater than ourselves** could restore us to sanity.

3. Made a decision to turn our will and our lives over to the care of **God as we understood Him**.

4. Made a searching and fearless moral inventory of ourselves.

5. Admitted to **God**, to ourselves, and to another human being the exact nature of our wrongs.

6. Were entirely ready to have **God** remove all these defects of character.

7. Humbly asked **Him** to remove our shortcomings.

8. Made a list of all persons we had harmed, and became willing to make amends to them all.

9. Made direct amends to such people wherever possible, except when to do so would injure them or others.

10. Continued to take personal inventory and when we were wrong promptly admitted it.

11. Sought through prayer and meditation to improve our conscious contact with **God as we understood Him**, praying only for knowledge of **His** will for us and the power to carry that out.

12. Having had a spiritual awakening as the result of these Steps, we tried to carry this message to alcoholics, and to practice these principles in all our affairs.

Once Bill W decided for himself religion was necessary for recovery, he had to figure out how to convince other skeptics this was true. He tackled this challenge most directly in the

"We Agnostics" chapter of *The Big Book,* the foundational text of AA first published in 1939, of which he was the primary author.

He begins this chapter by sharing that some members of the original AA fellowship were "violently anti-religious," and for others "the word 'God' brought up a particular idea of Him with which someone had tried to impress them during childhood." Essentially, he tells the religious skeptics: We were just like you. The difference is we are now sober, and you are not. "We found that as soon as we were able to lay aside prejudice and express even a willingness to believe in a Power greater than ourselves, we commenced to get results." In this way, he explained the importance of accepting a higher power in very practical terms. If a belief in God helps sobriety, we should believe in God.

Accepting a higher power might be a deal-breaker for many contemporary spiritual seekers, but not all. A 2023 survey by the Pew Forum found that a belief in God was quite common among folks with no religious affiliation or who did not consider themselves religious. According to the study, 20 percent of "spiritual but not religious" people believe in the God of the Bible, and 73 percent believe that there is "some other higher power or spiritual force in the universe." But what about those for whom, like my dad, God talk is a deal-breaker?

ED THE ATHEIST

Let's look at another of AA's early founders, who by his own admission caused a lot of trouble for the early fellowship. Though his real name was Jim Burwell, he was referred to in AA literature simply as "Ed the atheist." (My dad's nickname was also Ed, so for me, there are two people called "Ed the atheist.")

Burwell, who founded the first AA group in Philadelphia in 1940, participated in conversations about creating *The Big Book* in 1938–1939. He is best known as the person who insisted the phrase "as we understood Him" be added after the reference to God in the third and eleventh steps. My dad shared these concerns with AA's God talk, but unlike Burwell, he never figured out how to resolve them. What did Burwell discover that my dad didn't?

The story of Burwell's road to sobriety is included in *The Big Book* in a chapter called "The Vicious Cycle." It begins with what he calls his "D-Day," the day he hit rock bottom: January 8, 1938. His wife had left him, his landlord had thrown him out, and he had lost his job. "Thirty-nine years old and a complete washout," he writes.

That was when he learned of a group in New York made up of former drunks who had gotten sober. Willing to try anything, Burwell traveled to New York and began to attend weekly AA meetings in Bill W's Brooklyn home. His first impression of the group was that they were a bunch of "confused idealists." But the fellowship seemed to be working for them, so he decided to stay.

"I was a menace to serenity those first few months," Burwell confesses. During meetings, while everyone else shared their journey to sobriety, Burwell "took every opportunity to lambaste that 'spiritual angle,'" and "anything else that had any tinge of theology." Maybe others needed to be saved, but as Burwell wrote, "*I* was all right; *I* just drank too much." As he tells it, he decided to "take all they gave out with, except the 'God stuff.'"

My dad's experience with AA in a residential rehab center was similar. When we talked on the phone two weeks into his program, he described the other residents as "a bunch of screw-ups." They were much younger than he was and addicted to, in his words, much more serious things. Some were unable to hold a job, while he had been a successful corporate executive his entire life. Some had been arrested for disorderly conduct, domestic violence, or stealing to support their habit; he hadn't had so much as a parking ticket in decades. He told me he wasn't as bad an alcoholic as they were. "Dad," I told him, "I think you're a bad enough one," reminding him he was in a rehab program for a reason, which made him laugh.

But the distance he saw between himself and them was part of what allowed him to believe the religious content of AA was not necessary. Maybe the others needed that God stuff, but according to my dad, he didn't.

The AA God talk made it harder for my dad to work the program, just as it did for the other Ed the atheist, Jim Burwell. Burwell was able to get sober in the spring of 1938, but only temporarily. During a work lunch that June, he drank with some customers and then spent four days, in his words, "wandering around New England half drunk." But this new rock bottom seemed to have inspired him to soften his opposition to believing in a higher power. "My brilliant agnosticism vanished," he writes, "and I saw for the first time that those who really believed, or at least honestly tried to find a Power greater than themselves, were much more composed and contented than I had ever been." Burwell began to suspect that acceptance of a higher power was the missing link in his recovery.

At first, Burwell tells us, the only idea of a higher power he could accept was the power of the group. They had solved their alcohol problem, and he obviously had not; his June bender was evidence of that. In that respect they had a power greater than he did, and surely, he could at least believe in that. And then Burwell's understanding of higher power evolved. He mentions that when he started teaching others about the program, he began to warm up to the idea of God. In an article titled "Sober for Thirty Years," published in the May 1968 issue of *A.A. Grapevine*, he wrote that gradually he "came to believe that God and Good were synonymous and were found in all of us."

NOT-GOD

Bill W's personal God seems quite far from Burwell's understanding of a divine spark within each of us. That made me wonder: Did they share some core belief that was the key to AA's efficacy? If so, could it be useful to the quest for well-being even for someone who did not see themselves as struggling with addiction?

The first step to answering this question is to shift our focus a bit. Let's put aside the idea that accepting a higher power is about knowing or defining what that power is, and instead think about what it says about us. As historian Ernest Kurtz argues in his book, *Not-God*, AA's belief in a higher power is less about theism and more about the recognition that the alcoholic is himself "not infinite, not absolute, *not God*."

It is sort of strange that the fact that we are not-God is something we must learn, but the Enlightenment's hyperfocus on individualism really did a number on us. So, yes, I think this can be a useful takeaway from AA—not that we must believe that God exists, but rather that we must accept that we are not-God. We must give up on the delusion that we're in control. This is a religious idea, found in every religious tradition I study, which all teach the importance of decentering human agency, unsettling the notion that we're the most important thing in the universe, taking us down just a notch.

To say we are not-God is to admit we don't have all the answers and in fact in some ways are powerless. This understanding of higher power is accessible to even the most ardent skeptic.

Let's go back to *Griffin v. Coughlin*, the legal cases over AA-based programs in prisons. You might remember that I said I disagree that AA programs in prisons are a violation of the Establishment Clause of the First Amendment. Given what I've just said about the role of a higher power and religious experience in the AA program, how is that possible?

I'm sure it's clear at this point that I think AA has Christian religious roots and much of its rhetoric draws on Christian concepts and tropes. It was born out of the Oxford Group. There are references to God and higher power in the Twelve Steps. The stories of recovery in *The Big Book* often follow the arc of a Protestant conversion narrative. So no, AA is not secular, and that would mean that an inmate like Griffin would in fact be exposed to religion while participating in an AA meeting despite being himself an atheist.

But AA does not endorse one religion as better than others for recovery. What it endorses is the idea that *some* religion may be important to combating addiction, that religion is the "it factor" of sobriety. And legally speaking, some support of religion is possible without violation of the Establishment Clause, as long as one religion is not endorsed above others. Which is all to say that while AA might expose an inmate to religion, it does so in a way that allows for the self-curation that we think is so important to religious freedom in the United States. It advocates for religion but does not show preference or "establish" a particular one.

Was Griffin asked to recite the Serenity Prayer? Probably. Did some of the other members of the group describe their own journey to sobriety in religious ways? Likely. Was he exposed to theological ideas? Definitely. But all that means is that "religion was in the room." And I've got news for you: It almost always is.

THE ADDICT IN ALL OF US

In January 2024, I decided to try out Al-Anon, the sister organization to AA that caters to friends and family of alcoholics. According to the "Welcome Newcomer!" pamphlet I received at my first meeting, Al-Anon groups "are a fellowship of relatives and friends of alcoholics who share their experience, strength, and hope in order to solve their common problems." The organization has its own literature, such as *Paths to Recovery*, which lays out Al-Anon's Twelve Steps (to heal ourselves), Twelve Traditions (to build a healthy relationship with friends and family), and Twelve Concepts of Service (to extend what we learn into the world). Its motto can be summarized by its three C's: *I didn't cause it, I can't control it, and I can't cure it.*

As the child of an alcoholic, I'd avoided Al-Anon for years. I thought I didn't need it. If you remember, I began this chapter by saying that of all my struggles with well-being, addiction is not one of them. But I've come to see that is not exactly true.

The afternoon of my first meeting, I called a woman I'll refer to as Vicki, a friend of my parents' who I know regularly attends Al-Anon meetings. My plan was to get a primer on Al-Anon from her so that I would be ready to learn as much as possible from attending an actual meeting. Vicki has also known me since I was four, and knew my father well. The first thing she said was, "Liz, you are definitely a candidate for this group. Addiction has affected your life, whether you know it or not."

Wait a minute, I thought. *There's been some mistake.* I told her I was attending this meeting merely as research for my book.

But Vicki wasn't having it. "I think this could be really good for you. You might think, *Hey, this is interesting* if Researcher Liz shows up, but what if instead you just try to listen? I think you'll find out how much you do belong."

I was reminded of the time I went to a therapist in college because one of my best friends was bulimic and I wanted to learn how to help her, only to have the therapist ask about *my* relationship to food and body image, and why I felt it was my job to help my friend? I was furious at the therapist, who I thought had missed the point entirely. I never went back.

I wasn't mad at Vicki in the same way, but by the time we got off the phone, I was pretty nervous. The plan had been to attend an Al-Anon meeting as research. Now I was going to have quite a bit of skin in the game. Agitated, I changed my outfit three times before I left the house. What exactly does someone wear to a twelve-step meeting?

The meeting was about a mile away from my house in a church I knew as one of the distribution centers of the Brookline Food Pantry, where I volunteer. That made it a little easier to enter the large Protestant church. The directions on the website told me to walk up a few flights of stairs and head to the choir room, where I found a small sign on the door saying "Al-Anon meeting, all are welcome." There were five people already there who obviously knew one another and were casually chatting. They glanced at me when I entered and smiled, but no one spoke to me. The room was set up with twelve chairs in a horseshoe facing a big computer monitor with a Zoom room open. I put my coat down on a chair outside the horseshoe and pulled out my phone to check emails so I wouldn't have to make eye contact.

By the time the meeting started, we were nine in total: eight in person, one on Zoom. We began by going around the circle and reading the Twelve Steps out loud from a large poster set up behind the Zoom monitor.

The meeting facilitator, reading a script from a binder, asked if it was anyone's first meeting. I raised my hand and got some more smiles. "Would anyone be willing to sponsor her?"

he asked, still reading from the script. Three people raised their hands. I looked at my feet. An older gentleman was assigned as my sponsor.

Then we all picked up a copy of *Paths to Recovery* from a pile at our feet and started reading out loud again. Since it was the first week of the new year, our selection for the day was a chapter on Step One: "We admitted we were powerless over alcohol—that our lives had become unmanageable." I realized Step One was the "not-God" step of Al-Anon.

We read every line of the ten-page chapter out loud. In the first section, we learned "alcoholism is a family disease," because it "not only exists inside the body of the alcoholic, but is a disease of relationships as well." Vicki was right: I qualified for this group based on that criteria alone. In one of the chapter's personal stories, an Al-Anon member writes, "It took time for me to admit that even though I didn't drink the alcohol, the disease could come through me and affect other people. . . . My reactions to other things could be the same as the ways I reacted to the drinking." Could my dad's alcoholism explain some of my own patterns of behavior, like my anxiety when things aren't in my control?

The chapter ended with twenty-three questions to help us "work" this step. Number Twenty-Two read, "Am I attracted to alcoholics and other people who seem to need me to fix them? How have I tried to fix them?"

"See?" I imagined Vicki saying. "Al-Anon can explain why you went to therapy for a bulimic friend and why you dated all those tragic men you thought you could save in college."

As the child of an alcoholic, I thought it was my job to smooth out the rough edges of others. I thought if I was a good enough daughter, friend, partner, or mother, the people in my life would be healthy. And suddenly I realized addiction did affect my well-being, even if I didn't drink or do drugs.

Then it was time to share. Reading from the binder, our facilitator asked if any new members wanted to share. The woman sitting directly across from me saw me tense and very quietly said, "You don't have to." I said, "No, thank you." But everyone else, including the one woman on Zoom, shared for the three minutes the timekeeper allotted them. The whole point of the anonymity of the group is that I can't share the details of the stories I heard that night, but everyone mentioned who their "qualifier" was, whether a parent, child, or partner. Many shared the challenges they had just faced over the holidays. I'm ashamed to admit that I judged the others in the group just as my dad had judged others at his AA meetings. The phrase *I'm not like these people* ran through my head. But Vicki's voice was also there: *Remember, we are all like these people in some way.*

I didn't share that first night, but as I walked home, I allowed myself to imagine what I might have said.

> *Hi, I'm Liz. My dad is my qualifier. I'm not sure why I'm here. I'm not sure what I need. I lost my dad this summer to pancreatic cancer. His diagnosis is what finally got him sober. AA never worked for him, so I'm not sure Al-Anon will work for me. But it might. I thought that since my dad is no longer alive, alcoholism wasn't part of my life anymore. But this meeting made me realize maybe that's wrong. Maybe alcoholism is still here in behaviors that have nothing to do with drinking alcohol—at least not with* me *drinking alcohol—but are patterns I've learned. People-pleasing, a short temper, stress when I feel out of control. Maybe those are the effects of addiction on me. Maybe I am also in recovery.*

Overall, the meeting was easier than I expected. A large part of that was probably my conversation with Vicki. I was also relatively far into the research for this chapter, so I had already come to terms with the idea that the theism of AA could have meaning and utility without buying into Christianity.

But the religion of AA and Al-Anon was still uncomfortable for me. It was uncomfortable to enter a church for the meeting. It was uncomfortable to sit in a choir room and hear people sharing their experiences with addiction. It was uncomfortable to read out loud from an authoritative, quasi-religious text. It was uncomfortable to join hands to recite the Serenity Prayer.

But, following Vicki's advice, I sat with that discomfort and tried to not shut down. And that was how I started to really believe the AA God talk can be helpful to a religious skeptic like me.

RESTORING RELIGION TO AA

Many of us are seeking to tap into something larger than ourselves. AA does this for a lot of people, and it does so in part through religion. So the question becomes: What are AA's insights into well-being that might be helpful for those who don't want to embrace its Protestant roots? And could those insights work for those of us who don't struggle with addiction, at least in the traditional sense?

AA takes what scholars call a pragmatic approach to religion, so let me say a few words about what that is. I think it will be attractive to anyone who has trouble with the idea of religious belief or faith. I think it would have helped my dad work the program.

AA's pragmatism is inspired by William James—the only scholar Bill W cites in the entire *Big Book*. James was an American philosopher and psychologist whose 1902 book *The Varieties of Religious Experience* is a foundational text in the study of religion. In it, James focuses on actual human religious experiences of God, ignoring the debate so many Christian theologians were having at the time about the attributes of God. Is God trinity or unity? Is he all-powerful? Eternal? Immutable? Nonphysical? James basically said, *Who cares?* It wasn't that James didn't believe in God, because he did. He was just more interested in our concrete human experience of God. He focused on how religion shapes our everyday lives and assessed religious beliefs based not on if they were provable but on if they were useful to us. This is religious pragmatism.

When I say AA takes a pragmatic approach to religion, what I mean is that the program doesn't assume we need to know what God is, or even have conclusive evidence God exists, to accept a higher power. Instead, it suggests considering that a higher power might exist, and acting as if it does. It's not exactly *Fake it till you make it*—more like *If you believe it, you can achieve it.* If we believe that our lives can have meaning and live according to that belief, we might just discover that living in such a way can create the very meaning we're searching for.

Another way to think about this is that AA is nudging the skeptic toward an agnostic orientation (believing that nothing is known or can be known about God) rather than an atheistic one (believing that there is no God). And why not? If we don't have proof of the existence of God, we also don't have proof that God doesn't exist. And giving the idea of a higher power the benefit of the doubt allows you to work AA's program.

And if you do work the program, you'll see that AA has lessons about the human condition—the meaning and purpose of our lives in general—as well as how to think about well-being. Both stem from the religious insight that we are not-God. And even if AA is not a program widely suggested for everyone, like yoga or mindfulness, that doesn't mean we can't think about how to adopt aspects of its God talk to make our lives better.

AA points out that addicts try to manage the world around

them and suggests that this is pretending to be God. The first step of accepting a higher power is to recognize our own patterns of playing God. Because we all do it. Understanding that we are not-God reduces our "main character energy" a bit, removes us from the center of the universe, and deflates our ego. It puts us in our place.

One of my close friends in recovery describes addiction as a sense of feeling out of control, which creates a hunger—for a substance, a person, an activity—that is never satisfied. Being out of control seems to be a common feature of our contemporary lives. I feel out of control of my daughter's social media consumption, the mental health of my students, impending climate disaster, national politics, my back pain, the stock market.

And while an alcoholic tries to find temporary relief in a drink, others of us try to find it through wellness practices. We are convinced that if we just find the right product or adopt the right routine, we can look how we want to look, succeed at work and love, prevent disease, even stop the aging process. All of that is playing God. Sure, alcoholics experience a concentrated experience of addiction, but what I have learned from folks who have worked the AA and Al-Anon programs is that addiction is a spectrum, and there is an addict in all of us.

In my first Al-Anon meeting, I came to see another takeaway about well-being more broadly. Disease and disability aren't things that happen to other people. They do and will happen to all of us. We get sick. We experience loss. We age. AA makes space for the idea that human nature is fundamentally unwell. "Fallen" might be a Christian way of saying this. Augustine describes "bondage of the will." William James, "sick souls." Suffering, in this view, is not the exception in life, it is the constant.

Instead of *wellness as mastery of our lives*, I like the idea of *well-being as the process of recovery* that AA offers. This both acknowledges the vulnerability of human life and accepts that perfect self-optimization is not possible. Our goal, as Vicki told me, is to change the things inside the reach of our Hula Hoop—and to learn to accept that there are some things outside our hoop entirely.

One limitation with the Hula Hoop metaphor is that it doesn't have much to say about how we might have responsibilities to others outside our hoop, or how our hoop overlaps with other hoops. But AA does have insights into this as well. In fact, our acceptance of a higher power isn't only about a new understanding of ourselves as not-God. It is the first step to understanding that we are not alone, and that others are part of our journey toward real well-being.

As Bill W and Dr. Bob supported each other's sobriety, the AA program from its beginning has taught that fellowship is important to recovery. This idea has a couple of lessons for how to think about responsibility in the pursuit of well-being. For one, part of recovery is working to help others recover, as AA's Twelfth Step tells us: "Having had a spiritual awakening as the result of these steps, we tried to carry this message to alcoholics, and to practice these principles in all our affairs."

Put differently, service is part of the recovery process. I think this idea is often missing from the sorts of communities that pop up around wellness practices. A real community is not just about giving you a sense of belonging or providing encouragement. A real community often asks for something from you. It comes with obligations, not just support.

A real community often asks for something from you. It comes with obligations, not just support.

AA's understanding of fellowship goes both ways. We need to be willing not only to give but also to receive. And there is a cautionary tale here about the trap of trying to recover alone.

My dad probably fell into this trap. Sharp and witty, he was a chemical engineer by training who got all A's in college even though he couldn't afford to buy any of the textbooks. He was often the smartest person in the room, and he knew it.

Part of why AA didn't work for my dad was that he thought there was a lot of distance between him and others in the program. He felt the folks he met in rehab deserved his sympathy, but he didn't see them as his peers. Understanding that he was not-God might have come with a new level of humility and acceptance of just how much in common he had with other addicts. And that could have allowed him to learn from them.

But would any of these more religiously robust notions of purpose or responsibility really make AA work better? Or put differently, is religion (rebranded as spirituality to make it more accessible) part of AA's efficacy? A 2000 study in *Alcoholism Treatment Quarterly* reported that most AA members it surveyed—a whopping 91 percent—had had "a spiritual awakening" since joining the program. Several other studies have found that having a spiritual experience correlates with successfully working the AA program.

The AA founders thought a spiritual experience was important for sobriety as well. In fact, the point of all the God talk was to prepare us for such an experience. But what is it supposed to entail?

According to AA, you don't need a dramatic moment in which God speaks directly to you. The spiritual experience is more like a process than a lightning bolt. *The Big Book* assures us, "Most of our experiences are what the psychologist William James calls the 'educational variety' because they develop slowly over a period of time."

Burwell is an example of this. Bill W tells a very dramatic story about Burwell's aha moment in *Twelve Steps and Twelve Traditions.* Tossing and turning in bed, wallowing in the fact that he felt deserted, Burwell brushed his hand against a book . . . the Gideon Bible. And ta-da, he was saved! But this story was fabricated. Burwell's own account is far less dramatic—and more useful for us common Joes. In his article "Sober for Thirty Years," he writes, "I feel my spiritual growth over these past thirty years has been very gradual and steady."

If this sort of spiritual awareness sounds like something we might achieve by skipping all of AA's God talk, it is not, at least not for the founders. *The Big Book*'s appendix "Spiritual Experience" says this explicitly: "Most of us think this awareness of a Power greater than ourselves is the essence of spiritual experience." But rather than having our metaphysics completely sorted out, all we need to begin what will likely be a lifelong process is to understand something about ourselves—namely that we are not-God. And that seems like something even those of us who continue to reject a religious identity could get behind.

Of course, all of this is easier said than done. Imagine the alcoholic, or really anyone, who has hit rock bottom, needs help, and must now grapple with a core concept of a belief system—a higher power—that they have never accepted before. And now imagine they've had bad experiences with religion in the past, so that grappling with the idea of a higher power is also confronting a specific form of abuse or internalized guilt. Just like the Enlightenment's views of individualism have made it harder for us to de-center ourselves, some of our experiences with religion have made it harder to accept that it might hold anything positive for us.

My dad never got there. I think it boils down to him being unable to trust the idea that religion could have utility for him without irrefutable evidence of God's existence. Unlike James, he couldn't ignore the metaphysical debates, and that meant he never overcame his belief in the superiority of secularism. He was convinced he was better off than those who, as Bill W put it, are cracked about religion.

I think this is a challenge for a lot of us who don't claim a religious identity. We love to point out violence done in the name of religion, from the Crusades to clerical sexual abuse. We roll our eyes at religious moralists and fire-and-brimstone preachers. So much hypocrisy, bigotry, and corruption. But have we gloated at our own expense? "In belaboring the sins of some religious people," Bill W writes, "we could avoid looking at some of our own shortcomings. Self-righteousness, the very thing that we had contemptuously condemned in others, was our own besetting evil." The lesson here doesn't have to be "accept Jesus Christ as your savior," or even "start believing in God." It could be as simple as stop thinking you have all the answers.

I'm starting to get there, and AA's God talk has helped.

4

Eating Well

HOW RELIGIOUS FOODWAYS CAN HEAL TOXIC DIET CULTURE

Gwyneth Paltrow is an award-winning actress, but she is probably best known as a wellness influencer. Her lifestyle company, Goop, sells us things we didn't even know we needed through a sleek website, wellness summits, a print magazine, and a podcast. She is also the author of several well-produced cookbooks—I confess to owning one—that offer recipes and meal plans for "eating clean" or "detoxing." She herself follows an extremely strict diet. Just how strict, you ask?

In a 2023 interview with her personal "doctor," Will Cole (Cole is a chiropractor, not a medical doctor), she gives a play-by-play of what she eats each day—or more accurately, what she *doesn't* eat. "I do a nice intermittent fast," she starts off. Listeners can do some rough math and figure out that other than coffee in the morning, she appears to be fasting for eighteen hours a day. Lunch, her first meal, happens around noon. "I really like soup for lunch. I have bone broth for lunch a lot of the days," Paltrow tells Cole. She has an early dinner that follows the paleo diet, an eating plan that includes fruits, vegetables, lean meats, fish, eggs, nuts, and seeds, based on the theory that these were the foods that humans could get by hunting and gathering during the Paleolithic Era. Excluded from the paleo diet are farmed foods like grains, legumes, and dairy. This food plan, she says, is "really important to support my detox."

Even if this is an exaggerated self-report and she eats more than she says, presenting this as a healthy eating plan seems dangerous. It's not that bone broth or eating paleo are the problem—those are food choices that many people integrate into a healthy diet. It's that Paltrow presents her extreme caloric deficit as "healing" for various forms of inflammation she suffers from.

But undereating has serious health effects. It can weaken the immune system, making an individual more susceptible to illness. It can disrupt reproductive function, like ceasing menstruation. It can impair cognitive function and contribute to mental illness, like anxiety or depression. Malnutrition means a body breaks down its own tissues for fuel, including muscles such as the heart, leading to cardiac problems. It is linked to a higher risk of chronic diseases like diabetes, osteoporosis, and even cancer. And eating disorders have the second highest mortality rate of any psychiatric illness behind only opiate addiction.

The way Paltrow lays out her diet on this podcast was especially upsetting to me because more than one woman in my life has been diagnosed with an eating disorder. Both my sisters and my sister-in-law struggled with eating disorders as adolescents. One of my best friends in college was put on a psychiatric hold for one. My own daughter was recently hospitalized with life-threating bradycardia—her resting heart rate was in the thirties—after losing over 19 percent of her body weight in her junior year of high school. And this isn't uncommon. Nine percent of the U.S. population, or 30 million Americans, will have an eating disorder in their lifetime.

Although eating disorders are assumed to be a female disease, according to one study, 6.6 million men in the United States have experienced an eating disorder at some stage of their life. Extreme forms of male dieting have their own wellness influencers, especially among the brotastic biohackers of Silicon Valley. Jack Dorsey, the founder of Twitter, says he eats only one meal a day. This lets him feel, in his words, "much more focused." Bryan Johnson, the tech entrepreneur who claims to have the best biomarkers of anyone in the world and runs a longevity start-up called Blueprint, has his final meal at eleven o'clock each morning.

The goals of dieting might be gendered—thinness and beauty are offered as the feminine ideal, peak performance and longevity the masculine ones—but they have in common the idea that if we put enough effort into following an optimized diet, we can achieve a higher state of bodily perfection. And when you look closely, you notice that spirituality is frequently used to market new diets and food plans within the wellness industry.

I call these *spiritual diets.*

What do I mean by spiritual diets? Let's start by defining what they are *not.* Spiritual diets are presented as alternatives to the Standard American Diet (SAD), which is cheap and high in fat, glucose, processed foods. Spiritual diets claim to reject these things in favor of foods closer to their "natural state," which they claim are more nourishing for our bodies, save us from disease or even death, and help us obtain a sort of perfection that is often presented as thin and beautiful.

Spiritual diets come in several forms. There's the Paltrow version of pursuing wellness through dietary asceticism—in her case, reducing overall food intake. Often spiritual diets suggest not only restricting calories but also some form of fasting to "cleanse" the body of purported accumulated blockages or toxins.

Many wellness influencers preach the importance of eliminating foods deemed "polluting" or "toxic." Popular villains include gluten, soy, dairy, sugar, meat, and anything ultra-processed. More recently, seed oils, food dyes, and baby formula have become targets. All are said to contribute to unspecified inflammation, illness, and even death.

Other forms of spiritual diets focus on what you *do* eat: food that is organic, hyperlocal, vegan, raw, or caveman inspired. Some advocate for taking lots of supplements. They often mention the unseen "energy" of good foods, which they claim creates balance, prevents illness, and cures disease.

What does all of this have to do with spirituality or religion? A lot!

We might not realize it, but many of these extreme diets are influenced by decontextualized religious ideas about the body and food. Spiritual diets, for instance, tend to have three characteristics. First, they tend to be extreme, like Paltrow's and Johnson's diets, promoting forms of ascetism normally reserved for religious goals. Second, they often moralize food based on the idea of purity. And third, they tend to attribute dietary success—understood as thinness or avoidance of illness—not just to luck or genes but to a sort of secular piety, whether that is defined as self-control or craving only "healthy" foods in the proper amounts.

Put differently, diet culture has weaponized some religious food ideologies against us. It has confused a strict dietary moralism for an ethics of eating well. It has reduced food to individual optimization—whether that is conceived of as thinness or peak cognitive performance. And to do so, it has drawn on problematic religious ideas of food and body, while ignoring others.

In this chapter, I'll trace some current food fads back to older Christian anxieties about the body, pollution, and salvation. I'll also show how taking other religious advice about food more seriously can lead to a different understanding of what "eating well" entails and therefore inform our pursuit for well-being. My argument is simple: While spiritual diets rooted in religious language can perpetuate toxic diet culture, deeper engagement with religious foodways can offer healthier, more holistic alternatives to how we eat.

PROBLEMATIC CHRISTIAN IDEAS OF FOOD

Before I get to how religious understandings of food and eating can help us overcome toxic diet culture, let's first admit that religion, and particularly some strands of Christianity, has contributed to Americans' unhealthy relationship with food. I see three issues as the most problematic: asceticism, moralizing of food, and valorizing thinness.

Asceticism

Early Christians didn't advocate for the calorie-deficient diets aimed at thinness. But they were highly suspicious of bodily appetites like hunger. Many viewed the body as something to be overcome, connecting us more to beasts than to the angels we aspire to be. Augustine, for instance, believed the body could be a source of temptation and a hindrance to the soul's pursuit of spiritual perfection. And although fasting was established in the Mediterranean before Christianity, early Christians embraced it enthusiastically. Tertullian, a prolific Christian theologian from the second century who is considered "the father of Latin Christianity," believed that fasting countered Eden's primordial sin of eating the forbidden fruit. In the fifth century, Saint Jerome wrote that "the deliverance of the body from the encumbrance of much flesh" offered us "some conformity to God and his angels." It's safe to say that early Christians didn't embrace body positivity, and that their negative views on bodies sometimes led to ambivalence about food.

Anorexia nervosa is a relatively new disease, born in the nineteenth century, but food refusal in women goes back at least to the medieval period. Anorexia mirabilis, or "wondrous" restrictive eating, was practiced by medieval Christian women as a form of religious ascetism. Some took this to the extreme, rejecting normal food altogether and consuming only "the food of Christ" (the Eucharist wafers and wine) as their primary source of calories. Here the goal was not thinness or beauty but control of the body as a path to God, as historian Caroline Walker Bynum argues in her 1987 book *Holy Feast and Holy Fast.*

According to Bynum, these ascetic food practices were a form of female rebellion. Medieval gender expectations required women to marry and obey their husbands, and the gendered nature of religious authority limited women's participation in church leadership or ministry. These constraints stemmed from the perceived inferiority of female bodies—if male bodies were a problem, female ones were doubly so. Medieval women's fasting was an attempt to experience life beyond these femininized bodily restraints and thereby to escape that inferiority. In its extreme forms, as these women literally began to erase their bodies, it allowed them to avoid marriage, pursue public ministry, and challenge gendered religious authority.

Saint Catherine of Siena is a prime example. Born in 1347 in Siena, Italy, Catherine was a prolific writer of mystical treatises and prayers and took on the usually male role of pastoral care by feeding the poor and tending to the sick. She even became involved in church politics and is credited with convincing Pope Gregory XI to return to Rome, ending the period during which the papal residence was in France instead of Italy. In 1970, Pope Paul VI named her a Doctor of the Church, a title she shares with only thirty-six other saints, acknowledging that the Roman Catholic Church considers her works to be true and timeless.

Catherine's extraordinary life was possible because she was able to take monastic vows rather than marrying when she was young. Her family allowed this because she displayed exceptional Christian devotion, in part by practicing extreme food asceticism. At sixteen, her diet consisted of bread, water, and raw vegetables. At twenty-three, she gave up bread except for the Eucharist. By controlling her bodily appetites, Catherine presented herself as more holy than feminine, allowing her to circumvent traditional social norms such as marriage.

Catherine isn't a model for health and well-being; she died of starvation at the age of thirty-three. But the influence that gendered social pressures had on her eating habits does have some helpful insights into what is happening today.

Let me tell you a little about a friend I'll call Melanie. Melanie grew up in New Hampshire in what she describes as a conservative Christian family. She was diagnosed with an eating disorder in high school, after she passed out at a cross-country meet and was admitted to the hospital. She told me that at the time she was eating very little, purging, and overtraining. Decades into her recovery, she describes her restrictive eating as "a coping mechanism." "We were always this perfect Christian family," she said, and she was "the golden child," good at athletics, doing well in school. But that felt like a lot of pressure to Melanie. Despite the appearance that she was living up to the standards her family and church set for her, she felt very much out of control. "Eating was the one thing I could control," she told me. "I could control what I ate. So I ate very little."

What Melanie had in common with Catherine of Siena was that she felt the pressure of a gendered perfectionism, which, as historian Joan Jacobs Brumberg argues in *Fasting Girls*, "links personal salvation to the achievement of an external body configuration rather than an internal spiritual state." Anorexia mirabilis and anorexia nervosa are not the same thing, but both are symptoms of the unrealistic expectations put on women at specific times. Catherine of Siena's food refusal was a way to navigate the gender roles of her day by embodying the religious ideals of suffering and service. For Melanie, restricting food was how she coped with the burden of trying to be the perfect daughter.

And let's not leave out good old patriarchy. Both Catherine of Siena and Melanie were grappling with their exclusion from positions of authority and power and with attempts by others—family, institutions, men—to control them. And this of course turns out to be a problem not just for Christian or other religiously identifying women. As Joanne Grenfell, a bishop of the Church of England, writes, "The anorectic is refusing to take in other people's visions of who she is, the bulimic is vomiting out the intrusions of others, and the compulsive eater is attempting to control the world by taking it into herself."

But the problem is restricting food doesn't change those gendered norms; it surrenders to them. For instance, not much changed in Melanie's family after her hospitalization. She did meet with a therapist, but never a nutritionist or an eating disorder specialist—all standard outpatient treatment for anorexia and bulimia. She learned years later that her parents had her discharged from the hospital against medical advice, which is why she never went through the full refeeding protocol, because they thought the doctors—and Melanie—were being overly dramatic. "They were like, 'You're fine. Everyone feels like that about food,'" she told me.

Melanie's parents might have had so much disordered eating around them, they just thought it was normal, and a daughter with an eating disorder wasn't in line with their image as a perfect Christian family. A daughter who was deacon, a varsity athlete, a straight-A student, and yes, thin, was part of that image. A daughter who was making herself throw up was not.

Moralizing Food

Melanie blames her eating disorder in part on the way food was categorized as good and bad in her home. Her mom would constantly say things like "I'm not going to have bread because it's fattening," and a healthy meal was defined as just salad and chicken. Melanie's family wasn't exceptional in this way. Since at least the nineteenth century, Americans have been moralizing food in conversations about health. And religion had a role in popularizing this problematic approach to food as well.

Religious studies scholars like to draw on the work of British anthropologist Mary Douglas to make sense of the food restrictions found in many religious traditions that rest on concerns with pollution. In Douglas's 1966 book, *Purity and Danger,* she argues that religious notions of dirtiness and cleanliness, or pollution and purity, are never quite as simple as what is and is not hygienic. These designations rest on what I described as worldviews in chapter 2, particularly assumptions about the proper order and purpose of things. Something is impure or dirty, according to Douglas, if it is out of place.

> *Shoes are dirty not in themselves, but it is dirty to place them on the dining table; food is not dirty in itself, but it is dirty to leave cooking utensils in the bedroom, or food bespattered on clothing. . . . In short, our pollution behavior is the reaction which condemns any object or idea likely to confuse or contradict cherished classifications.*

Douglas is pointing out that what we consider to be clean is sort of arbitrary. It is not about "dirt" but about the violation of a classification system. We get anxious when the rules we make to organize the world are broken.

Let's look at a case in which religious conceptions of pollution get applied to food in a broader cultural context. Sylvester Graham, a Presbyterian minister, was an early advocate for the idea that eating only "good foods" was necessary for physical and moral health of every American, not just Christian ones. During the cholera outbreaks of the 1830s, Graham began preaching about a vegetarian, whole-grain diet. Conventional medical advice at the time was that consuming meat and wine would prevent cholera. Graham believed that these foods were overly stimulating and encouraged disease. He suggested that Americans give up meat, eat vegetables, and bake their own bread. Butchers, bakers, and doctors opposed his ideas, but Graham used his preaching skills to convince many that he had discovered the key to dietary preventive medicine—including his namesake invention, the graham cracker. When cholera reached the United States in 1832, his followers fared better than most, which helped the idea that a vegetarian diet was healthier get a foothold in the American psyche.

Douglas's theory explains why Graham promoted his specific vegetarian whole-grain diet over one with meat—he thought meat was polluting and homemade bread purifying. It also helps explain modern spiritual diets that center on detoxification and cleansing. Take Paltrow, for example, who presents some foods (like bone broth and steamed vegetables) as good, and others (like pasta and cheese) as bad. This not only moralizes entire categories of food but also makes statements about cleaning toxins based on unscientific notions of pollution—Paltrow's *beliefs* about pollution, if you will. (As nutritionist Karen Reyes explains, "Our kidneys and liver have been created to do all the clearing we need without fad diets or restrictive eating habits.")

A common anxiety that grounds spiritual diets is that much of our food is polluted. It is full of chemicals, or genetically modified, or ultra-processed. This is presented as the result of industrial food production—or, if you believe folks like Vani Hari, aka "Food Babe," that our food is intentionally poisoned by big corporations.

And this distrust of our food often leads us to equate "natural" with "pure." Consider the wellness influencers who advocate for drinking raw milk. Raw milk has harmful bacteria that pose a significant risk of containing pathogens like salmonella, *E. coli*, and listeria. But since pasteurized milk has been heated to kill harmful bacteria, it is, from these influencers' point of view, less "natural," and thus more dangerous.

As Susannah Crockford, an anthropologist who studies New Age spirituality, writes, "The renunciation of various categories of food in the spiritual diet is similarly a religious act of purification. It is a way of keeping out the harmful aspect of the environment." Put simply, the condemning of specific foods as bad and the guidance to "eat clean" is based on a quasi-religious theory of pollution and purity.

Valorizing Thinness

Catherine of Siena restricted her food, but her goal wasn't thinness, it was devotion to God. Sylvester Graham promoted the idea of purity through physical and moral health, but his recommendations weren't aimed at weight loss either. Popular fixation with thinness came much later. And religion was part of that story as well. By the twentieth century, a robust Christian diet industry had emerged in which being skinny was not only more attractive, it was the only way to get to heaven.

Let's look at Gwen Shamblin, one of the best-known Christian diet gurus of the 1990s. A size-four woman with teased blond hair, Shamblin spoke with a Dolly Parton twang and offered up a Christian weight-loss program with pithy one-liners like "nothing tastes as good as skinny feels." A trained dietician, she drew from her own weight-loss journey to help others. After gaining weight in college, she says she "prayed to God for wisdom." God answered. "The scriptures and understanding started coming in little by little," she said, "and I started incorporating this into the original Weigh Down Workshop," a twelve-week program launched in 1986. Within ten years, the program was offered in five thousand churches. Shamblin published *The Weigh Down Diet*, selling millions of copies.

Shamblin had a specific theology of weight loss. She believed God created humans with two empty places—the stomach and the heart—and that each had a different "hunger." Weight problems occur when we try to fill the heart with food that goes to the stomach, otherwise known as emotional eating. Overeating, then, is based on a fundamental misunderstanding of human nature. Even worse, it's a form of idolatry, because it ascribes a transformative value to food that it lacks.

The solution offered by the Weigh Down Diet wasn't strict rules or calorie counting, but a biblically infused version of intuitive eating. Shamblin encouraged individuals to rely on their God-given internal cues to eat smaller portions. Eat only when hungry, stop partway through a meal, sip beverages slowly, consider eating only half of what's on your plate. Unsure how much to eat? Pray about it.

Weight loss is a journey, she said, like the biblical Exodus story. Just as God rescued the Israelites from slavery, God could rescue us "from the love of food and therefore, the unwanted pounds." The goal was thinness, but not only thinness. It was also about reaching heaven. "Fat people don't go to heaven," she famously declared.

Shamblin's wasn't the only Christian diet—the popular Daniel Fast, a twenty-one-day partial fast based on the biblical story of Daniel, comes to mind—but her assertion that fat people don't go to heaven did find a foothold. Melanie told me Shamblin's ideas were prominent at her conservative Christian college. Thinness was a sign that you were "taking care of your vessel that God gave you to be on this earth" by eating the right things in the right amount. "It was really shameful to not be a super skinny woman there," she told me.

Catherine of Siena, Graham, and Shamblin raised different concerns about our eating habits. For Catherine, restricting food intake was pious. For Graham, specific foods were sinful. For Shamblin, overeating was. However, taken together, Catherine's asceticism, Graham's moralization of food, and Shamblin's valorization of thinness all got adopted into a broader spiritual diet culture that implies that fat people aren't only unhealthy but also sinners, that most of our food is polluted and thus the cause of sickness (instead of nourishment), and that a perfect diet can lead to the perfect body (or a way to transcend it).

Here's where things get even dicier. Catherine's asceticism, Graham's moralization of food, and Shamblin's concerns with weight were all based on specific Christian beliefs of their time. But they became integrated into spiritualized and even secular understanding of food and health. Paltrow takes an ascetic approach to food and valorizes thinness, even though she would likely never say her food habits are based on Christianity. Robert F. Kennedy Jr.'s campaign against seed oils and food dyes might not be presented as a holy war against "unnatural" foods, but that's what it is. Melanie grew up in a Christian household, so she can blame her eating disorder on the conservative Christian beliefs of her family. But my daughter, who struggles with anorexia, did not. And yet she has also internalized the belief that some foods are bad for us and that she "should" have the willpower to eat less.

Since I know religion is already influencing how we think about food and wellness, I wondered, could it offer resources for thinking differently about food and well-being?

AYURVEDA'S ADVICE ABOUT HOW TO EAT

I began looking for religious conceptions of food that are more conducive to real well-being, particularly approaches that considered *how* food is consumed to be just as important as *what* food is consumed. And given how problematic Christian beliefs about food and the body have been in American diet culture, I thought non-Christian approaches to food could offer a different perspective. And that was how I ended up at an Ayurveda workshop for weight loss in the Berkshires.

That workshop wasn't my first choice for a deep dive into Ayurveda. I had initially considered doing a *panchakarma*, an intense Ayurvedic purification therapy that is the very definition of a cleanse and detox. The full treatment takes a month. Many folks travel to Ayurvedic institutes and ashram settings in India to complete it, but with a little digging, I found a program at an ashram in Grass Valley, California. To make the experience more feasible for those of us with jobs or families, this panchakarma began with a period of preparation at home, followed by about a week at Grass Valley for more intense treatments at the ashram. That seemed doable. I signed up for a Zoom information session with the program's supervisor.

The supervisor opened the session with a mantra and would close it with a short prayer. She explained that panchakarma was a practice going back five thousand years and would help rid our bodies of toxins that cause disease. The program would take five weeks. At home, we would spend three weeks eating a diet only of kitchari (a porridge of rice and lentils) and ghee (clarified butter), consuming whatever herbs the doctor prescribed, taking a daily steam bath, and practicing self-massage with oil.

The second stage was more intense. It involved ten days at the ashram, staying in a basic cabin while undergoing various purgation treatments, including five enemas. The supervisor explained that traditional panchakarma included induced vomiting and bloodletting, but that these aren't legal in the United States. That was a relief.

The final stage involved continuing mild treatments and rest at home. The overall goal was to remove deep-seated toxins. But it was an intense process, akin to surgery, she said.

When I asked if we would be learning about how to eat after the cleanse, I was told that was not a central part of the program. Panchakarma, at least this version developed for an American consumer, was a reset, an intense detox to put us back on track. I was much more interested in the lessons the tradition might have for staying on track in the first place. Panchakarma, at least as a one-off "cleanse," felt like another example of how religion can *harm* our relationship with food.

I went back to the drawing board, looking for an alternative way to learn more about how Ayurveda conceptualized foodways through the lens of Eastern worldviews and what suggestions it might have for approaching how I should eat.

I found a more accessible program nearby at Kripalu Center for Yoga and Health, located in the Berkshires. Two Ayurvedic practitioners were hosting a five-day workshop called "Ayurveda and Yoga for Healthy Weight and Wellness." I worried this title meant the leaders were assuming weight was a marker of health. Would I find a Shamblin-like thinness ideology here as well? But I figured this program would certainly emphasize an Ayurvedic approach to food. Since no enemas were mentioned in the program description, I signed up. Here's what I learned during the workshop and subsequent research.

Ayurveda is a complex system, a "science of life," offering information on disease prevention and treatment. It encompasses topics from psychology to surgery, so much of its content is relevant to wellness. While not a religion itself, Ayurveda is intimately connected to ancient Indian beliefs that predate Hinduism, such as Vedic religion, Vedanta, and Samkhya. I think of Ayurveda as a system that puts these belief systems into practice in order to foster a healthy life.

Classic Ayurveda scriptures describe four structures of the body: *doshas* (energies), *dhatus* (tissues), *agni* (fire), and *malas* (waste). Health is achieved when all these components are balanced. The workshop I attended focused on the impact food consumption has on the doshas.

In Ayurveda, doshas are the body's organizing energies. We all possess three—*pitta*, *vata*, and *kapha*—but are born with a tendency toward one or more (a doshic constitution). Lifestyle choices and seasonal changes can get our doshas out of whack. Understanding both one's natural doshic tendency and one's current imbalance determines the most nourishing foods for an individual.

According to an Ayurveda consultation I paid for a couple years ago, I have an excess of pitta, which is composed of fire and water elements that are associated with digestion and transformation. Excess pitta can lead to behavioral issues (short temper, frustration, competitiveness, criticism) and physical symptoms (heartburn, skin irritation, sweet cravings, inflammation). This describes me to a T.

According to Ayurveda, if you have a pitta constitution but are balanced, meaning that you're not experiencing the aforementioned symptoms, you don't need a special pitta diet. However, if your pitta is elevated, a pitta-pacifying diet might help. That would involve consuming foods with qualities opposite to those of pitta to restore harmony. Pitta-pacifying foods are mild, cool, dry, and slightly heavy (such as rice cakes), tasting sweet, bitter, or astringent (such as arugula).

But these qualities can also depend on how food is prepared. The example we talked about during my workshop was eggs. Hard-boiled eggs have a different quality (thick and heavy) than scrambled eggs (soft and warm). And the addition of spices can also change the qualities of food. Cardamom, cilantro, coriander, fennel, and mint are said to have cooling qualities to help calm pitta's heat. Those with pitta imbalances are also advised to avoid aggressive conversations during meals, eating while angry, or eating too quickly—all of which can increase your pitta.

Because Ayurveda developed within a religious context that emphasized how the qualities of food influence internal states, its recommendations are not simply about eating "good" and avoiding "bad" pitta foods, but rather about eating what's appropriate for you at a particular time in a particular way. And the goal of eating well in this system is not thinness or cognitive optimization. It is achieving a sattvic state of balance and harmony.

In his book *Eating Ethically*, religious ethicist Jonathan Crane identifies three characteristics of healthy religious eating that help explain the Ayurvedic approach to food: savoring, sharing, and sacrificing. Ayurvedic savoring involves eating without distractions. Think no screens, a quiet environment, eating slowly, taking deep breaths before eating, noticing the food's qualities, and expressing gratitude. In terms of sharing, Ayurveda points to the benefits of positive social interaction during meals. The system also emphasizes sacrificing for healthy eating. Snacking is discouraged, as regular mealtimes are thought to help balance doshas. Instead of calorie counting, Ayurveda practitioners rely on a natural burp, indicating fullness, as the sign to eat no more at a meal.

The Ayurvedic advice, in a nutshell, is that savoring, sacrificing, and sharing our food is just as important for eating well as meeting our daily nutritional goals. Yes, it's true that Ayurveda would recommend that I not eat spicy food when I'm experiencing a pitta imbalance, but not because spicy food is "bad." It's just not appropriate for me if I'm in that state. In fact, for someone with a vata imbalance, spicy food might be just what's needed. In this system, food is a source of nourishment that can create balance if we let it. This view avoids moralizing entire categories of food or shaming us based on our cravings. These cravings are symptoms of imbalance, and food is the medicine to fix that.

According to some researchers, adopting an Ayurvedic approach to eating might even have measurable health benefits. For instance, in a 2021 article in *Medicina*, Archana Purushotham and Alex Hankey, a neurologist and a biologist, compared two studies on the impact of vegetarianism on heart and brain health. The first was a massive eighteen-year study of over 48,000 participants in the United Kingdom, which found that vegetarians had a 22 percent lower rate of heart disease compared to meat eaters—but a 20 percent increase in stroke risk. By contrast, a separate study of about 18,000 participants over a period of five to seven years in Taiwan found a significantly lower stroke incidence among vegetarians—about 50 percent lower overall and 74 percent lower for ischemic strokes.

Why the radically different findings about the influence of vegetarianism on strokes? To find the answer, Purushotham and Hankey began by looking more closely at the specific foods consumed by participants in each study. The most striking difference they found was that the UK group consumed higher amounts of soy products and legumes. Western nutrition, with its focus on vitamins, minerals, and macronutrients, wouldn't see the source of plant-based protein as significant. So the researchers looked elsewhere, to Ayurveda, to help explain why the consumption of different types of plant-based protein in the United Kingdom and Taiwan might explain the difference in stroke outcomes.

As we discussed earlier, Ayurveda views disease as resulting from doshic imbalances, with each pathology linked to specific doshas. Food qualities either boost or suppress doshic function, directly affecting chronic illness. Heart disease is a kapha disorder; meat, with its grounding qualities, increases kapha. Ayurveda predicts that vegetarian diets reduce kapha disorders like heart disease—as both studies showed.

By contrast, Ayurveda links strokes and neurological disorders to chronic vata overload. And so Purushotham and Hankey asked: Did the UK vegetarian diet that was high in soy products and legumes create a stroke-inducing vata imbalance? Their answer was yes. As they explain, "In general, legumes . . . greatly increase *vata dosha*. Indian . . . vegetarian diets . . . favor the less *vata*-genic ones." The researchers also point out that from the Ayurvedic point of view, how plant-based protein is prepared matters. To mediate legumes' effect on vata, they can be rinsed, soaked, sprouted, boiled, and prepared with specific spices. This turns out to be how legumes are commonly eaten in Taiwan, where they are liberally spiced and cooked over a long time.

The UK vegetarians, according to Ayurveda, were doing vegetarianism incorrectly. And these studies raise the possibility that Ayurveda offers insights into how eating well might entail more than hitting Western science-based nutrition guidelines.

HOLISTIC FASTING DURING RAMADAN

Wellness influencers often promote various versions of fasting, claiming that not eating for long periods of time helps with weight loss, mental clarity, general inflammation, and unspecified toxins. Several religious communities encourage fasting as well, but usually with very different goals. Let's look at fasting during Ramadan, a widespread practice within the Muslim community, even among Muslims who don't consider themselves orthodox in other ways. Can a deeper understanding of this form of ritual fasting help us think differently about the benefits of restrictive dieting to our well-being?

During the month of Ramadan, Muslims abstain from food, drink (yes, even water), and sex from dawn to sunset. At sunset, the daily fast is broken with a celebratory meal called *iftar*, often shared with family and friends. Considered one of the five pillars of Islam, fasting during Ramadan is obligatory for those who are able, based on the Quranic verse 2:183, "You who believe, fasting is prescribed for you, as it was prescribed for those before you, so that you may be mindful of God."

But while classic sources are clear that fasting is an obligation, exemptions from fasting are built into that obligation. For instance, Quran 2:184 states that those who are "ill, or on a journey" can make up the fasting days later, and "for those who can fast only with extreme difficulty, there is a way to compensate—feed a needy person." The rationale for these concessions is explained in 2:185: "God wants ease for you, not hardship. He wants you to complete the prescribed period and to glorify Him for having guided you, so that you may be thankful." This echoes a central Islamic teaching that God provides guidance for Muslims in ways that are merciful, not punishing.

Since Muslim Americans are not immune from the influence of diet culture, some do hope to shed a few pounds during Ramadan. But few Muslims would claim weight loss is the primary reason to participate in holy fasting.

The Quranic verse 2:183 describes the purpose of Ramadan fasting with the Arabic word *taqwa*, translated as "being mindful" or "having awareness" of God. One way to understand taqwa is as the Muslim version of acknowledging a higher power discussed in chapter 3. But it is much more than that. Taqwa is the way of living that results from this awareness, a commitment to an ethical life out of responsibility to God. During Ramadan, the individual restrains bodily appetites for things like food in order to focus inward and draw closer to God.

There is also an element of personal moral training that can occur during the sustained fasting of Ramadan, much like the embodied virtues taught through devotional yoga, as discussed in chapter 1. On an episode of the podcast *How God Works*, Khalil Abdur-Rashid, a scholar of Islamic studies and Muslim chaplain at Harvard University, describes the first level of fasting as staying away from food and water. But, he says, there is a second level to fasting, which is regulating our emotions to improve our interactions with others. "If somebody is trying to pick a fight with you or argue with you, you're supposed to respond by saying, I'm fasting." If you're fasting from food but losing your temper with those around you, you're not really engaged in what he calls "holistic fasting."

Generosity is the most common virtue I hear associated with Ramadan. The experience of discomfort from hunger, thirst, and sexual abstinence during Ramadan is said to foster empathy, not just sympathy, for those who are less fortunate. Almsgiving and volunteering is encouraged as an expression of this generosity.

A study out of Baylor University attempted to measure increased levels of several virtues during Ramadan among two hundred observing Muslim adolescents. Researchers hypothesized, for instance, that a habit of patience was created during Ramadan because the month requires "the ability to remain calm in the face of frustration and deprivation." And in fact their study did find that teenagers self-reported being more patient during Ramadan. And interestingly, although to a lesser degree, they thought they had more patience even when the holy month was over.

Finally, fasting during Ramadan builds community and family ties. For a 2019 study, researchers interviewed forty-seven Muslim families living in the United States on the role of family during the month of Ramadan. Some interviewees mentioned how breaking fast together every day meant more time for family discussions, others how getting up very early to have a pre-dawn meal strengthened family ties. Researchers noted that their interviewees didn't refer to Ramadan as an individual practice but rather as an experience they did as family: "We sit together, we eat together, and we pray together."

Kirsten Wesselhoeft is a scholar of contemporary Islam

studying Ramadan observances among Muslims in New York who are ambivalent about organized religion. While they may not be showing up at weekly services or praying five times a day, and they're skeptical about the version of Islam they were taught as children, many still observe Ramadan. When I asked her why, she said on one hand it's about the rigor, and on the other hand, it's about the party. "I think the fact that it's super hard is part of what keeps people anchored in the practice. It's a discipline that makes you reorganize your life a bit," she said. But these young Muslims also love how fun and communal Ramadan is. During the holy month, you can show up at any Muslim space and there will be people sharing food. As Wesselhoeft put it, "Every night for thirty days, you can go to a dinner party."

Anyone who has observed Ramadan can tell you that it's at least as much about eating as it is about fasting. And Ramadan's approach to food has a few broad insights into the role of eating for well-being that might be useful to non-Muslims as well.

The first lesson is that food is meant to be shared. That is why the fast is broken with a communal iftar. Eating well is not eating over the kitchen sink, in front of the TV, or in our cars during a daily commute. Eating well happens when we eat with others.

Eating well happens when we eat with others.

The second lesson is an important corrective to early religious devaluations of the body. The Ramadan body is not the shameful and sinful thing Augustine or Shamblin thought we needed to restrain, or the weak and flawed containers the tech bros are trying to biohack themselves out of. It is an important vessel for religious insight. As Wesselhoeft put it, "Our bodies are the way that we connect with one another and the way that we connect with God." You can't successfully fast without a body, after all.

A third lesson of Ramadan is that eating well, or successfully not eating during a ritual fast, is not really the goal—it's the means to much more ambitious ends. Al-Ghazali, the prominent eleventh-century Islamic thinker, explained this nicely in *The Mysteries of Fasting.* "It is clear, then, that every act of worship is possessed of an outward form and an inner [secret], an external husk and internal pith," he said. In Ramadan, fasting from food is merely the external husk. "It is for you to choose," al-Ghazali wrote, "whether to be content with the husk or join the company of the wise and learned." A larger takeaway could be that controlling the body through a specific diet is always just the husk. We would do well to consider the more important internal pith our food practices are aiming to change.

Observing Ramadan with an Eating Disorder

This all sounds pretty good, but I also want to acknowledge that because there is so much focus on food during Ramadan, it can be a challenging time for Muslims with eating disorders. For an individual not yet in recovery, communal fasting can mask disordered eating. For someone who is newly diagnosed, restricting food might set back their refeeding program. For those further along in their recovery, ritual fasting can trigger a relapse. An iftar featuring large quantities of delicious and rich food can be challenging for those who have bingeing and purging tendencies.

I spoke with Dr. Rania Awaad, an Islamic teacher and clinical psychiatrist who leads the Stanford Muslim Mental Health and Islamic Psychology Lab, about this issue. She explained that although the food restriction of fasting at Ramadan and eating disorders may look similar, their intentions are very different. "A lot of times, the purpose behind somebody restricting with an eating disorder has a lot to do with body image," she said. "Sometimes it has to do with food textures and such, but usually it has more to do with restricting for weight loss."

In contrast, during Ramadan, Awaad said, "we fast in order to experience." The point is to really feel what it's like to be hungry, because that hunger can make clear the position of comfort and privilege we normally occupy and make us more likely to want to help others who are less fortunate. Dr. Omara Naseem, a London-based eating disorder psychologist, addresses the issue of intention in her guide for observing Ramadan with an eating disorder. An eating disorder, she writes, can prevent Ramadan fasting from having its intended benefit because it may "skew your mindset away from faith and more towards fasting for the eating disorder (e.g. to lose weight)." If you're fasting to lose weight, you're not doing it for God.

Dr. Awaad thinks religion should help guide medical recommendations for a patient observing Ramadan with an eating disorder. "I have found that clinicians don't have the answers, and religious leaders don't fully have the answers," she told me. "Because I'm trained in both—I'm a faith leader and I'm a psychiatrist—I realized my perspective was different than most." She understands the health challenges to fasting with an eating disorder, but she also understands that observing Ramadan has benefits that might be crucial to a Muslim patient's well-being. This has led her to conclude that recommendations can't be the same for everyone.

Awaad points out some eating disorders are acute and some are chronic. For someone who has lived with an eating disorder for decades, Awaad thinks it's important to ask them how they have observed Ramadan in the past. "Have you fasted for the last thirty years? And have you done okay with it?" These are important questions to ask before telling a patient not to fast. In more acute cases, "maybe a patient has just been hospitalized and maybe they have a lot of other medical conditions that are because of their eating disorders." In those cases, Awaad thinks it would be counterproductive to fast, not only from a medical point of view but also from a religious one. "Risking one's health," she says, "would not be seen as meritorious nor commendable in Islam." In cases where fasting is not medically recommended, Awaad is clear that the religious exemption from fasting for illness applies.

Luckily, in Islam, there are alternatives to fasting during Ramadan. Naseem and Awaad both mention a few. In a nod to the Quranic suggestion to feed a needy person, they suggest helping to prepare the iftar meal, but they also add other options that don't have anything to do with food, such as maximizing time for worship, committing to reading a passage of the Quran every day, listening to lectures or podcasts about Islamic teachings, spending time with one's family, or donating to support one's community.

I think there is a broader lesson from Ramadan that can help counter extreme diet tendencies, even outside the Muslim community. Ramadan isn't about fasting as much as possible for as long as possible. There are boundaries put on how many hours people fast (sunup to sundown) and for how many days (one month). There are a lot of reports of the Prophet Muhammad correcting someone who tries to extend their fast by fasting even longer. Wesselhoeft recounted one for me during our conversation.

> *There's a hadith about Muhammad approaching one of his followers who he's heard is fasting outside of Ramadan, staying up*

> *all night to pray, like really pushing these ordinary acts of worship to a kind of level of asceticism. Prayer and fasting are in general good for people. Muhammad is trying to get people to do these things. But this guy is like, "I want to be so good that I'm doing these things all the time." So Muhammad goes to him and says. "I hear that you are fasting all the time, and then you're praying all night." And this guy is like, "Yes, I am doing those things." And Muhammad says, "Don't do that. Fast sometimes, and then other times don't fast. Pray at night sometimes, and then don't pray on other nights. Your body has a right over you."*

On one hand this is a hadith cautioning us about too much of a good thing. Sure, praying is good, fasting is good, but doing them all the time doesn't make them work better. Attempting to be overly pious is counterproductive.

But there is another insight here, and one that might be harder to accept because of deep-seated beliefs that the body is flawed and thus an obstacle to our well-being. It is that every bodily urge isn't a problem to be solved. When Muhammad says, "Your body has a right over you," Wesselhoeft told me, he means "even in what you feel is like an abundance of enthusiastic piety, you are not allowed to ignore the needs of your body." Meeting bodily appetites, including hunger, is also part of well-being.

RESTORING RELIGION TO FOOD

The moral question is not, according to the famous philosopher Jacques Derrida, "Should one eat or not eat, eat this and not that?" but instead, "How for goodness' sake should one eat well?" Since food is a common way religions think about and cultivate well-being, it is worthwhile to consider how they offer ways to heal our disordered relationships with food.

But as we've seen, religious approaches to food are not

inherently benign. The restrictiveness of Catherine of Siena's diet, Sylvester Graham's moralization of food, Gwen Shamblin's shocking declaration that fat people won't go to heaven, and the induced vomiting of panchakarma—these approaches to eating all strike me as extreme. But the problem isn't their religious content, per se. The problem starts with extracting religious ideas and practices from broader contexts and then using them to justify a specific diet. It is time to take a step back to consider what we have learned from a more robust understanding of religious approaches to food that can make eating more meaningful, responsible, and effective.

In religious traditions, food can express relationships with the cosmos, maintain worldviews, create connections to divinity, symbolize a group's history, and reinforce communal identity. They encourage us to think about *how* to eat, not just *what* to eat. This is why, instead of "religious diets," scholars have suggested the term "religious foodways" as a more accurate way to think about the ways religions approach food.

Religions see everyday practices like eating as opportunities to remake ourselves into different people. I like how Elizabeth Pérez, author of *Religion in the Kitchen*, a book about food in the Santería tradition, puts this. Preparing food, she says, gets "under the skin of practitioners, equipping them with the repertoire of skills, dispositions, and habits necessary for religious norms to be internalized and then reproduced." Ayurvedic eating practices assume food is a dharma-ordained substance, and thus that eating well is a path toward enlightenment. Ramadan fosters individual virtues like generosity and patience, as well as behaviors toward others based on these virtues, like volunteering and not losing your temper.

The takeaway here is that eating is a way we can put our values into practice, strengthening them by literally "taking them in" through consumption. None of that is possible unless we first make sure our foodways are consistent with those values. And that requires being clear that food is more than calories, macros, and other nutrients. Food is a moral substance and, if approached well, is nourishing for body, mind, and soul.

In fact, it seems to me that religious foodways are at their best when based on morality instead of moralism.

Religious foodways are at their best when based on morality instead of moralism.

Advice from wellness influencers about food is often very individualistic, promoting the idea that if you eat the correct foods in the correct amounts, *you* (and you alone) will be saved. In contrast, many religious practitioners approach eating as a way to connect with others and believe eating well requires a community to break bread with. We have all experienced the joy of a shared meal. This is an important reminder for our well-being. You might achieve some level of wellness alone, but real well-being depends on your connections to others. If we were able to think about food as something with ramifications beyond ourselves, it could go a long way toward healing our relationships with food.

This doesn't have to look like a communal Ramadan iftar. For example, some people refrain from meat out of respect for the moral standing of animals; others eat locally to reduce their environmental impact. We might each ask ourselves, What forms of social or environmental responsibility do I want my diet to reflect? How might my food be an opportunity to think and act socially?

In the examples of Ayurveda's approach to food and Ramadan's ritualized fasting, we see that the religious contexts might matter in terms of the risks and benefits certain eating practices provide. The scientific study about strokes and vegetarian diets implied that eating a meatless diet within the full Ayurveda worldview was quite different than in a secular Western one. Those two versions would view protein sources differently, emphasize the role of food preparation differently, think about the importance of the baseline constitution of an individual differently—and as a result, maybe even differently affect our cerebrovascular health. And the example of observing Ramadan with an eating disorder raises the possibility that the context and intention of restricting food changes its effects on a person's well-being. Fasting within the context of an Islamic ritual to become more empathetic is very different from limiting food intake within the context of mainstream diet culture to lose weight.

Another insight from religious foodways is that we should think about the benefits of eating well beyond a number on the scale or BMI. What would a more robust measure of effective eating look like? Eating that gave us the same level of energy all day? Eating that led to stronger social bonds? Eating that was pleasurable, joyful, and without guilt? Eating that encouraged sustainable farming practices?

And finally, holistic religious foodways encourage a shift away from the idea of eating as an avenue to bodily perfection. It is tempting to think we can solve all our health problems with the right food plan. But there is no diet that can make us perfect. And we will never be skinny enough, pretty enough, live long enough if our goal is perfection.

5

Spiritual Fitness

MUSCULAR CHRISTIANS, INSTRUCTOR GURUS, AND THE MAGIC OF BELONGING

I booked my first SoulCycle ride with "Kelly," who had a reputation as the hardest instructor in the Boston SoulCycle scene. A friend who was an experienced rider joked that if anyone could convert me to the lifestyle, it would be Kelly.

The morning of my class, I dressed in the most coordinated thing I could find in my collection of workout clothing, shoved my Peloton shoes into a tote, and headed to the Chestnut Hill studio three miles from my house. When I arrived, I found a lot of women and a few men. Most were wearing SoulCycle merch, and several had purchased SoulCycle-branded boxed water for $5.50. My outfit and Nalgene looked sad in comparison.

I tried to shake off the feeling that I didn't belong and focus on figuring out how SoulCycle was using spirituality to sell me wellness. One way was obvious: its name. Certainly, the word *soul* meant I could expect something more than a good sweat. But there were other signs too. The "Sanctuary Manifesto" was written on the wall, promising an inclusive and welcoming space. "Whoever you are, however you feel, wherever you come from, whatever you look like, you belong here." All souls are welcome. The word *sanctuary* also evokes a sacred space—or maybe an alternative to one. This sanctuary was consecrated not by holy water but soulful sweat. When I entered the spinning room, it felt like entering a church. The lights were dim, and a grapefruit-scented candle was burning. The bikes were set up like pews with a raised altar in front.

A cheerful employee helped me find and set up my bike. I climbed on and began to slowly pedal. Kelly sauntered in, greeting the riders in the front row by name. The lights went down, the music turned up. And we began our forty-five-minute class.

We spun our feet chasing a beat. We rode flat roads, then climbed imaginary hills by turning the resistance knob further and further to the right. We bopped side to side. Tapped our butts back and thrust our hips forward. Completed a series of pushups on the handlebars. Kelly reminded us the hills were metaphors for struggles we have in life, and as we built physical strength, we were also building emotional and spiritual resiliency. We chased the sense of release, the feeling of catharsis, the hit of post-workout endorphins. The atmosphere was energetic. We were the fitness equivalent of a revival, hooting and hollering, swaying to the music with our eyes shut.

As the pace of the class picked up, Kelly shouted mantras at us: "We inhale intention and exhale expectation!" We breathed deeper. She told us to open our chakras, and although I wasn't sure what she meant, I tried to do it. We were told to feel the energy, to manifest, to self-actualize, to live our most authentic lives.

I had thought SoulCycle would be my sort of thing. I've taken group fitness classes since middle school, starting with VCR tapes of Jane Fonda and Solid Gold dancers, moving to health club cardio and strength classes in the 2000s, and pivoting to livestreamed HIIT classes during the pandemic before fitness influencers decided they raise our cortisol levels too much. I have a Peloton bike and a Concept2 rowing machine parked in my guest room and a set of weights in my office. So if any popular wellness technique could help me find true well-being, I thought it would be a spiritual exercise program. It certainly personally appeals to me more than any other technique in this book.

But while the SoulCycle ride did ask a lot of me physically—I was out of breath, overheated, and dripping in sweat by the end—it didn't feel like a serious container for self-transformation. I wasn't even sure I was on board with the type of change it assumed was "good." Kelly's sermon at the peak of my first SoulCycle class was a good example. During our last long climb, she told us to listen to the lyrics of the song that was playing, which were something about giving up the last seat on a plane. "Think of who you love enough that if there was one seat left on a plane, you would give it to them." This was the big crisis she had come up with to teach us about sacrifice? Giving your seat to your BFF when the flight back from your vacay in Tulum is oversold?

When I left the studio after that first class, I recorded a quick video to post on social media saying I didn't know why people got addicted to this class. "I feel like I was just yelled at in the dark for forty-five mins, and I paid for it," I said.

A friend who is also a former SoulCycle instructor saw my

post and DMed me immediately: "I'm just cracking up that you hated it. My first class I thought Jesus was there and I had been saved. LOL best 45 mins of my life."

No one invited Jesus to my first ride. There was obviously something I had missed. This chapter is about trying to figure out what that was.

I use the term *spiritual fitness* to refer to a group exercise class, whether held in person at a studio or livestreamed online, that claims to offer not only physical but also spiritual self-transformation. For the most part, these programs pair movements—sometimes quite intense movements like heart-pumping burpees, fast pedaling on a stationary bike, or martial-arts-inspired punches—to raise our heart rates and fatigue our muscles. Get people in a zone of physical and emotional exhaustion, and then the real training begins.

Once we're worn down, the instructor offers some sort of "sermon" or leads the group in affirmations spoken in unison. Crying is encouraged as cathartic. Testimonials of how the routine "saved me" are commonly offered. And suggestions about how to embrace ourselves as worthy and show up differently in our lives are offered. The idea is that we leave one of these classes having achieved not only a good caloric burn but also something more profound, whether that be an emotional release or a new way to value ourselves.

It's not so much that I think these workouts are religious per se, or that they are necessarily appropriating from specific religions—although in some cases they certainly are. Rather, I think they're functioning like religion in people's lives. And by looking at them through the lens of religious studies, we can understand better how these workouts are a form of "well-being training," if you will, how they might work better, and even what insights they have for folks who don't want to combine a fitness routine with their spiritual growth.

THE RELIGIOUS HISTORY OF SPIRITUAL FITNESS

Physical regimes have a long history as religious devotional practices. Sweat lodges. Daily prayers that involve physical prostrations. Breath control as a technique of spiritual work. And sometimes these exercises can be quite punishing, such as Native, Christian, and Muslim ceremonies that involve self-flagellation.

Long before it was standard medical advice to say exercise is needed for our health, which didn't happen until the 1950s, there were religious beliefs about physical fitness as part of wellness. In fact, exercise's earliest advocates in the United States were not physicians but Protestant intellectuals who framed exercise as part of moral training and preached the importance of fitness for a righteous Christian life. It was this religious framing, not a scientific discovery of exercise's physiological benefits, that seeded the popular idea that a fit body is a good body.

Muscular Christianity and the YMCA

Christian support for exercise wasn't always the case. Early Christians saw the body as an impediment to the salvation of the soul. It needed to be controlled, and all fleshly desires quashed. In fact, there could be no important role for exercise in any Christian theology that emphasized predestination, the idea that whether we're going to heaven is determined by God before our birth. Nothing we can do will change the fate of our soul, least of all exercise. It is fair to say that for much of history, Christians saw exercise as misdirected because it focused on strengthening the unruly body instead of the spirit; it might even be immoral, because it could be motivated by vanity and self-gratification.

But a new theological movement in the nineteenth century set the stage for the promotion of fitness regimes as part of spiritual growth. This is when we see the emergence of what the health historian James Whorton calls the "crusaders of fitness." These reformers were concerned that men were becoming soft from urban living and that Christianity was becoming feminized. They decided the solution was for men to act more manly. They should spend more time with other men in fraternal lodges and engage in physical activity to strengthen their bodies. This movement came to be known as "muscular Christianity."

Advocates of muscular Christianity pointed to the Bible as proof that a good Christian man was a fit one. They highlighted 1 Corinthians 6:19–20, which discusses the importance of physical health, and Mark 11:15, in which Jesus literally flips a table, thereby sanctioning physical displays of male power and aggression.

Muscular Christianity promised that if men became more fit, it would strengthen the nation and attract more young men to the church, rebranded now as an institution of male virility. And women weren't left out entirely. Advocates of muscular Christianity would encourage women to exercise so that they could conceive and birth more children. Although muscular Christianity would eventually be adopted by some Black Christians during the civil rights movement as a method of self-empowerment, in the beginning, muscular Christianity was a way for white Christians to continue to enjoy power. More manly white men and more fertile white women would help reinvigorate the declining British Empire's dominance.

Preaching that physical fitness was necessary for salvation required a significant theological move away from the idea of predestination and toward the idea of self-determination—that an individual's actions decide their fate. Once that move was made, salvation was understood as coming only to those who earned it through right living. The logic went something like this: Since nature was good, human bodies must also be basically good and intended by God to be healthy. If someone wasn't healthy, it was because of their own bad choices. Illness, weakness, even fatness became not just physical problems but also spiritual ones. This new Christian theology shifted the responsibility for our wellness squarely onto our shoulders.

You might never have heard of the muscular Christianity movement, but it's a big part of the origin story of the YMCA—and I bet you've heard of them, and maybe even worked out at one of their gyms. Founded by a group of evangelical Christians in the United Kingdom in 1844, the Young Men's Christian Association was originally conceived of as an alternative to saloons, dance halls, and brothels for young men. By offering a space for prayer meetings, Bible studies, and practical services like housing and employment listings, the YMCA aimed to help convert young men and keep those who were already Christian safe from the temptations of urban life. YMCA clubs began to open in the United States in the 1850s.

If YMCA had stayed focused on male bonding and proselytization, there might never have been a SoulCycle. But a major shift occurred in the late 1880s when, under the leadership of L. Wilbur Messer, the YMCA moved away from evangelization toward promoting a Christian lifestyle for young urban men. Given the influence of muscular Christianity at that time, a strong body was seen as one way to build a strong Christian character, and so the YMCA began to make physical fitness central to its mission. It rented athletic fields and swimming pools and then built its own. It developed bodybuilding programs, and created new sports like volleyball and basketball, all to cultivate good Christian values and character traits in its members. The fact that volleyball and basketball originated at the YMCA blows my students' minds! Whether in K–12 sports programs, national leagues, or even the Olympics, the popularity of athletics is evidence of just how mainstream the ideas of muscular Christianity became.

The YMCA, or "the Y" as it's commonly called today, is the most successful gym franchise ever in the United States. It began as an explicitly religious institution with a religious mission and only took off when it shape-shifted to be accessible to non-Christians. And that is not a coincidence. The Y's belief in the virtue of exercise was based on the Protestant theology of muscular Christianity, but it went mainstream when those religious origins were secularized into "morality," "lifestyle," and "wellness," giving it a broader appeal.

Phineas Parkhurst Quimby and New Thought

There is one more religious movement that paved the way for spiritual fitness by popularizing the idea that positive thoughts can lead to physical health. When your fitness instructor tells you to manifest your best life by rescripting your self-talk, they are drawing on an idea with roots in the nineteenth-century Christian mind-healing movement known as New Thought.

Let's look at Phineas Parkhurst Quimby, one of the founders of the New Thought movement. In the 1830s, Quimby became a practitioner of mesmerism, or animal magnetism, a new occult trend that was sweeping Europe and the United States. Founded by the German doctor Franz Mesmer, it was a healing system based on the belief that all living creatures have a magnetic fluid that could be controlled by the mind for healing purposes. When Quimby encountered mesmerism, he thought he had rediscovered Jesus's healing method. All those miracles in the Bible? To Quimby, they were examples of Jesus learning to control the magnetism in the world.

The New Thought movement began to teach that positive thoughts could heal us. It was the nineteenth-century version of "good vibes only." Over time, the explicitly Christian foundations of New Thought have faded into the background. What remains are its ideas that positive thinking, mantras, and generally controlling our minds can affect our physical health. And certainly, this grounds much spiritual fitness, such as a SoulCycle instructor's cues to feel the energy in the room, set an intention, and manifest the future we desire.

The story of muscular Christianity, the YMCA, and New Thought shows how the marriage of religion, physical movement, positive thinking, and health is not new. There is a long history of theological justification for value-informed physical fitness as a pathway to morality and salvation.

What is new since the 1990s and 2000s is the explicit marketing of fitness brands like SoulCycle as spiritual but not religious. Muscular Christianity and the New Thought movements were explicitly Christian, as was the YMCA when it was first established. But today, popular spiritual fitness brands don't tie themselves to one tradition. They are based on the idea that their spiritual content is acutely effective but also universalizable and accessible to all, so it can be offered in ways that avoid the sectarianism of organized religion. "SBNR fitness," if you like. And despite proponents' insistence that these forms of spiritual exercise have left behind the baggage of religion, they still function like religion in people's lives.

CHARISMA AND FITNESS GURUS

Instructors play a central role in popular spiritual fitness programs. They draw us in and keep us coming back. And the concept of charisma can help us understand how this dynamic works.

I began my academic career thinking about charisma. My dissertation at the University of Chicago's Divinity School focused on an unlikely pair: Pope John Paul II and Ayatollah Ruhollah Khomeini, who both wielded enormous charisma in ways that had profound effects on Catholic and Shiite communities respectively. For that work, I read tons of scholarship on charisma from my field, most of which draws on the work of German sociologist Max Weber. Little did I know that what I learned would be helpful decades later to make sense of the fitness instructor as a combination of prophet and celebrity.

For Weber, charisma comes in different forms. He acknowledges those with a sort of natural-born charisma, the "bearers of specific gifts of body and mind that were considered supernatural." Prophets and popular religious leaders, like John Paul II and Ayatollah Khomeini, have this sort of charisma. So do celebrity fitness instructors. Jack LaLanne, Jane Fonda, Kathy Smith, Chuck Norris, Richard Simmons—all became household names and built exercise empires of workout videos, books, and training plans based in part on their natural charisma. They were attractive based on modern standards of beauty, but more than that, they attracted us with their personality and presence. They had some quality that made others want to be like them, follow them, get close to them.

When you combine the charisma of a religious leader with the charisma of a fitness instructor, you get a fitness guru.

When you combine the charisma of a religious leader with the charisma of a fitness instructor, you get a fitness guru—a spiritual exercise trainer who offers a transformation not only of the body through movement but also of the soul through spiritual wisdom. These aren't mere boot-camp drill sergeants with fitness know-how who provide guidance on how to do physical movements. That is the least of their job. Through sermons, eulogies, confessions, and witnessing, they inspire, build connections, appeal to our values. They are preacher, therapist, friend, life coach, and sex symbol all wrapped into one.

One of SoulCycle's founders, Julie Rice, was a talent manager, which is likely why the company realized the importance of charismatic instructors from the very beginning. The brand recruits for star quality, preferring to hire those with a performance background, like dancers or actors, or folks who had large social media platforms with proven track records of building a following.

One former instructor I spoke to described the first round of the audition process as like being a contestant on *American Idol.* Fifty wannabe instructors in a studio, each already a SoulCycle devotee, each who now wanted to give this experience to others from the front of the room. SoulCycle had changed their lives, and they wanted to share that with others. It felt like a calling. Some planned to quit their jobs as hairdressers and lawyers if they made it; others would drop out of school. Everyone was in full makeup and dressed in SoulCycle-branded attire, leading a mini-class during which they tried to prove they could be inspirational and aspirational, spiritual and physical exemplars. The goal was to find instructors so appealing that riders would do anything to attend their classes. "If people aren't obsessed with you," a former SoulCycle instructor told me, "you're doing it wrong."

Stacey Griffith, the SoulCycle celebrity instructor, is a great example. She has been teaching for the brand for almost two decades. Her classes are regularly sold out. But Stacey's popularity isn't based only on her high-energy choreography. She offers riders a powerful conversion story as well: Spiritual exercise saved her, so it can certainly save you. As she writes in her memoir, *Two Turns from Zero*, "All my years of addiction, and all my experiences in life, are a huge part of why I am as successful as I am as a teacher. . . . I am living proof that you can recover and detoxify and cleanse and clear and become a totally different person."

Although we think of charisma as a special quality in a person, Weber's second insight is that charisma is a two-way street: It depends on a community that recognizes that charisma. For instance, a charismatic religious leader's power depends on (a) followers' belief that the leader has a special connection to the divine, (b) an emotional connection between the leader and their followers, and/or (c) the leader's message resonating with their followers. In other words, someone is a charismatic leader only if they find the right group that will respond to their particular form of charisma.

This is also true for spiritual fitness gurus. Stacey became a celebrity instructor in part because she was filling a need among her followers—a desire to lose weight, feel more powerful, find connection, heal from an eating disorder, recover from addiction, remake themselves inside and out. She was tapping into something that already existed.

While charisma is powerful for building a religious or fitness community, it also poses a challenge: It is hard to sustain beyond a founding charismatic leader. If that leader dies, quits, or otherwise leaves the picture, the movement is at risk of falling apart.

Religious communities have tried different paths for transferring power. Sometimes the leader identifies a successor—for example, Shiite Muslims believe this was the case with the Prophet Muhammad and his son-in-law Ali, whom they consider the first imam. Sometimes a leader's bloodline is understood to contain the charisma. But more common is locating that charismatic authority in a particular institution or office.

This is a third insight from Weber that is helpful to us. Although charisma can be wielded by an individual (for example, a prophet), it can also be "routinized" so that it lives beyond the life of that figure. Take the example of the Catholic Church I first studied in graduate school. Obviously, Jesus wielded tremendous charismatic authority for his followers. After his death, that charisma continues for Catholics to some extent in the office of pope. This is why a modern pope who does not have much personal charisma—I'm thinking of Benedict XVI, who was not particularly popular among Catholics—can still wield tremendous authority. Charisma is why religious institutions are so important. They establish positions of charismatic authority—the pope in the Roman Catholic Church, the ayatollah in Shiite Islam, the Dalai Lama in Buddhism, and the patriarch of Constantinople in the Eastern Orthodox Church—so that leadership can continue and the community can survive.

Fitness brands that begin with celebrity instructors also have to figure out ways to do this. For a group spiritual fitness class, instructor charisma is what keeps us coming back week after week. Even if I wasn't a fan of Kelly's SoulCycle class, it was clear others there were. They were booking a bike every week to ride with her. They were convinced she was the instructor who could help guide their wellness journey.

I didn't respond to Kelly quite that way, but I did to Stacey Griffith when, in spring 2023, I booked the last bike available in one of her classes at the Eighty-Third Street studio in New York.

Stacey made quite the first impression, sauntering into class late in a neon tank and joggers, and yelling at us, "I'm back!" having just been on vacation. Hoots and hollers of appreciation came from around her room. And then we got down to business.

"Turn that dial three clicks to the right. Get up, get on the beat," Stacey coached from the floor, pacing back and forth in front of us. For most of class, I couldn't see her, but that didn't matter, she told us. "Follow the front row," she yelled several times, referring to her self-designated disciples. "That's what they're for, that's why they wanted to be on those bikes."

As a workout, those forty-five minutes were the best experience I'd ever had at SoulCycle. I pushed myself harder than I had in any previous spinning class, because I could see how hard everyone else was pushing themselves. I finished exhausted, my clothing soaked, endorphins pumping. It made me want to book another ride with her. It made me want to be part of her squad.

But at the same time, I found something about the class unsettling. I think it was because of the assumed values of the group. Let me give an example. Stacey made several references over the course of the class to "haters" on Reddit who didn't want her to "talk about bodies," saying things like, "If they're talking about you behind your back, it's because you're two steps in front." During the last song, she screamed, "I'll never stop teaching!" The room erupted in cheers.

When I asked my research assistant to look into it, the only thing she found was a Reddit user who criticized Stacey for mentioning losing weight for an upcoming wedding. This seems to be the comment that had offended Stacey, but from my experience, Stacey *did* have a body-focused dogma—Thou shalt look good in a bikini by summer. And even though I had cheered her, and even waited around after class for her to sign my copy of her book, a beach-ready bod isn't really what I was looking for in an exercise class. And yet I had gotten swept up by Stacey's charisma.

I don't blame Stacey for any of this. She is obviously a talented and dedicated fitness teacher, and I respect her journey from addiction to sobriety. But if spiritual fitness classes are supposed to transform us, we need to be aware of what sentiments and values ground a particular vision of transformation.

This means it is important to evaluate whether a spiritual fitness program is the right fit for us. What sorts of transformations do participants report having? What core values are part of a particular brand? How is wellness defined? Reflecting on those questions are how I decided SoulCycle isn't quite the right fit for me. So, I went back to the drawing board.

THE EVOLUTION OF INTENSATI

I'm in my home office, shouting affirmations into a Zoom room while trying to execute various aerobics, kickboxing, and yoga moves. "Eight, seven, six, five, four, BRAVE!" I yell as I punch my hands over my head. "Eight, seven, six, five, four, ABUNDANCE!" I say as my hands open into a wide V over my head. "I am braver than I seem! I am blessed with all I need!" I repeat mantras with their corresponding moves and then yell, "Just think it!" I'm doing a spiritual fitness method called intenSati. I can feel my partner rolling his eyes at me from his office on the floor below. Even the dog looks concerned.

You've probably never even heard of intenSati, unless you happened to attend Equinox on the Upper West Side in the early 2000s, where ten classes a week were filled with stressed-out New Yorkers completing a series of moves paired with positive affirmations. According to the promotional materials currently on its website, intenSati was "the original spiritual fitness method." This is sort of true. Certainly, there were mash-ups of exercise and religion that predate it, like the forms of exercise that sprang from the muscular Christian movement. And there were also "religious versions" of popular fitness programs, like PraiseMoves, "the Christian alternative to yoga," that were created over concerns that movement classes like yoga were dangerous missionary arms of New Age spirituality, paganism, or Eastern religions.

But all of that is quite different from intense fitness programs claiming to have serious spiritual content but open to anyone, independent of religious affiliation. And even if you've never heard of intenSati, it predated SoulCycle by four years. It was the first in the genre I'm referring to as spiritual or SBNR fitness.

The first thing I did when I started a deep dive into intenSati was read its founder Patricia Moreno's book, *The intenSati Method: The Seven Secret Principles to Thinner Peace.* That was not a good place to begin. This book was written in 2010, before Moreno herself fully rejected the ideal of thinness as a marker of health, and many of the affirmations she offers in the book are focused on self-control around food choice. When I first took my intenSati class via Zoom, I couldn't shake the idea of it as a technique for "thinner peace." It certainly didn't feel transformative in a good way to me.

But people I respect—like fitness historian Natalia Mehlman Petrzela, whom you'll hear more about later—adore the program, so I knew there had to be more to the story. Unable to find an in-person class in my area, I decided to just jump into the deep end and enrolled in an intenSati teacher training. I also interviewed long-standing members of the community, both teachers and students, trying to figure out why intenSati worked for so many people.

The first thing I learned was that the fatphobic origins of intenSati are a holdover from Moreno's childhood and the 1990s fitness industry she was part of. They are not core values of the program today. And then I began to understand that intenSati was revolutionary when it started and has evolved over the last decades to become something different, but no less radical.

Moreno's own story of spiritual fitness salvation began when she was put on her first diet at the age of eight. When she reached 212 pounds at the age of twelve, her mother took her to a weight loss specialist who injected her with cow's urine to speed up her metabolism. She spoke candidly about how doctors, diets, and constantly being weighed and measured left her feeling full of shame and convinced that her weight was the result of not having enough willpower. In other words, Moreno was the victim of the toxic diet culture and fatphobia I discussed in chapter 4.

Things begin to change for Moreno when, at seventeen years old, she walked into her first Jazzercise class and immediately fell in love: "I loved dance, movement, the music, and the community. I felt free and empowered. . . . I wanted to preach and teach about the benefits of exercise and to help others fight their fat." And that is exactly what she did, at least at first.

It's important to understand what was going on in the fitness industry as Moreno began her journey to become a fitness instructor. Group fitness classes were wildly popular, and their aim was unapologetically weight loss. Most fitness was framed as chasing a bikini body or earning your dessert. Working out was penance for overindulging the night before.

Powerful, graceful, and a creative choreographer, Moreno excelled in that climate. Her classes became known as exceptionally challenging. She won fitness competitions. She was regularly featured on the early morning TV program *Breakfast Time*, and she had sponsorship deals with Nike, Reebok, Everlast, and Danskin. She trained fitness instructors around the world. She became one of the most popular and highest-paid instructors at Equinox in New York City. In the 1990s, she was, by all measures, a fitness star.

But all wasn't as it seemed. In her words, she felt like a fraud: "I was muscular and sometimes lean . . . but I still felt out of control." She might have been preaching the importance of diet and exercise for changing your life to packed classes, but that formula wasn't working for her. She was struggling. Sometimes barely eating. Sometimes purging. Even taking crystal meth to curb her appetite. She was burnt out, depressed, and addicted. And that was when she realized the standard way of thinking about fitness wasn't the path to well-being after all.

Moreno started looking for a new path. She tried different forms of movement like yoga. She read best-selling self-help books by Deepak Chopra, Wayne Dyer, and Abraham Hicks. She explored life coaching. Amid this searching she found herself in the Bahamas attending a Tony Robbins retreat. While walking on the beach with hundreds of participants chanting, "All I need is within me now," she had her aha moment: "That's it! A workout with affirmation! The missing piece! The mindset! It is not what we're doing, but the mindset from which we're doing it that determines our failure or success!" In other words, fitness classes might work a lot better for herself and others when paired with positive self-talk.

And thus, intenSati was born. The name is a combination of the English word *intention* with the Pali word *sati*, which is usually translated as "mindfulness" (a topic I discussed in chapter 2). During a class, high-energy moves—inspired by kickboxing, aerobics, and dance—are paired with high-emotion mantras. So imagine students powerfully punching while saying, "I believe I will succeed," each word getting its own punch. Or pulsing a squat to "every single day I value myself in every way." The goal is to train us to replace our negative self-talk with a more positive storyline. For many, it was a very emotional experience. Moreno told *The New York Times* during an interview in 2022, "If people are crying, you're doing your job right."

During my intenSati teacher training, Lucy Osborne, who was Moreno's business partner and now runs intenSati, describes how the practice instills new beliefs. "We have been doing a form of intenSati unconsciously our whole lives," she told us, "moving in a certain way and repeating negative mantras over and over again. Mine was *I'm not thin enough, I'm not thin enough, I'm not thin enough. I'm not good enough, I'm not good enough. I'm not worthy enough. No one wants me.*" intenSati is a training program for more than the body; it also retrains our inner running commentary. We are strong. We give love and receive love. We accept ourselves exactly as we are.

Learning the method during the teacher training was one thing, but I hadn't been able to take an in-person class, so I couldn't fully grasp what it felt like to practice intenSati in a group. To get a sense of this, I spoke to two women who took Moreno's classes at Equinox to ask them more about her, her class, and the community she created.

The first was Natalia Mehlman Petrzela, the fitness historian and author of *Fit Nation.* I knew of Petrzela before we met over Zoom, because she is what I'd consider a celebrity historian. She's a tenured professor, columnist, host of acclaimed podcasts, History Channel commentator, and all-around Wonder Woman whose life seems full of work, adventures, family, and friends. So I was a bit surprised to hear that she credits intenSati for her success. "When I'm being my best self," Petrzela told me, "I'm channeling that Patricia energy and that unapologetic exuberance."

Petrzela's own relationship with fitness goes back to her teenage years, when she attended her first step aerobics class at her local Jewish fitness center to get out of mandatory high school PE classes. In 2005, she met Moreno and discovered intenSati. At that time, Equinox was the fanciest gym one could join in the city, which meant Petrzela wasn't really considering it. But during an informational session, the membership director told Petrzela, "I'm going to give you this week pass, and you need to go to as many Patricia Moreno classes as you can. I promise you, you are going to figure out why you should join this gym."

At first, Petrzela took every class Moreno offered except the weird spiritual one called intenSati. Kickboxing, dance, aerobics—she loved them all and thought, *This woman could teach tax accounting and I would go to her class.* So she decided to try intenSati. She didn't say a single affirmation during her first class. But by her second class, she started to try them out, and then she noticed something: "I wasn't complaining about my dissertation as much. I was getting so much done. I was so much more optimistic." Overall, "I was getting better," she told me.

She began to plan her work schedule so she could make it to as many of Moreno's daily intenSati classes as possible. Eventually, Moreno convinced Petrzela to get trained to teach, and she became a much sought-after intenSati instructor at Equinox, second in popularity only to Moreno herself.

I asked Petrzela what she thought drew people to Moreno. Petrzela said Moreno wasn't like any fitness instructor she had ever met. The industry standard at the time was thin, small white women. Moreno was a "6 foot tall Mexican-American Amazonian princess" who was graceful but also big and strong. She was also always talking about how she struggled with her weight. Although today it's common to hear a fitness instructor sharing their personal life and struggles, it wasn't back then. This was years before the oversharing ethos of Instagram and Facebook. It felt revolutionary that Moreno would show up and talk about her personal problems. That vulnerability was part of her appeal. It made it clear she was in the work, just like her students.

For Petrzela, the physically demanding nature of the intenSati class was also important. The only way she could get on board with all the self-improvement stuff, she told me, was because the class was so hard. "Too often, the self-help world is kinda soft and lazy," she told me. But intenSati was different. "It was self-improvement, but not soft. Disciplined. Hardcore."

I asked her something that I was curious about: How did she get over the initial embarrassment of yelling affirmations in a public fitness class? Always the teacher, she reminded me of the historical moment she discovered intenSati. As she describes it, in New York City from 2005 to 2015, there was this fervor around wellness that felt new. "It was before every Target pillow had affirmations on it," she told me. "It felt exciting to hear this stuff and feel this stuff in that particular environment. It felt like we are on the cutting edge of something." Moreno was exceptionally charismatic, but she also found a community who was eager for what she could offer.

The next intenSati veteran I spoke to was Soul Camp founder and author Michelle Garside, whom I met when we were both students in the same intenSati teacher training. When Garside discovered intenSati in 2011, she was doing global brand development for Big Pharma at a large advertising firm. She was successful at her job, but unsatisfied. Then she found intenSati, and she changed everything. She quit her corporate job, starting shopping at Whole Foods, joined Equinox, and attended an intenSati class every single day.

For Garside, intenSati was special for slightly different reasons than it was for Petrzela. While Petrzela described Moreno's charisma in terms of her physicality—so big and strong and graceful—Garside describes it in terms of love. "I'm not a devotee of Amma," she said, referring to an Indian guru known as the "hugging saint," "but it's a similar energy." She also mentioned Richard Simmons. "He was the embodiment of love, and no matter what your weight was, he loved you and you could feel that," Garside said. "It was the same with Patricia."

An even more striking difference is the role "exercise" plays in spiritual fitness for Garside compared to Petrzela: "To be honest with you, I didn't even care about the fitness aspect. . . . Sure, it's good exercise, but it was so much more the community for me." When I asked her what was so special about the community, she said it wasn't that this community was made up of perfect, shiny, happy people. In fact, the opposite: "Everyone had some kind of eating disorder recovery story like me." It was a group actively working on accepting and loving themselves. "I immediately had that feeling of belonging, of being accepted," she said.

The difference in how these two women describe what makes intenSati special is reflected in changes to the brand as well. From 2002 to 2019, Moreno had an exclusive deal with Equinox, a high-end wellness corporation, to teach intenSati at their gyms. And the focus during those years was very much the body and fitness. Folks like Petrzela came for the hardcore workout and got the other emotional benefits almost by mistake.

But over time, Moreno became more critical of the diet and fitness industry. She began to see the spiritual coaching of intenSati as just as important as its physical rigor, and she wanted more people to have access to it. As a result, the types of people drawn to intenSati began to shift. More folks like Garside found intenSati, often through word of mouth. They came for the sense of belonging and self-transformation. And the physical workout sometimes became a by-product.

A NEW DAY FOR INTENSATI

When Lucy Osborne took her first intenSati class in 2013 at Equinox, this shift was just beginning. By the time she became Moreno's business partner in 2017, the two of them began to realize that intenSati could, and maybe should, exist outside of the gym and started to think about how to market the training as "not (just) a fitness training."

By 2019, it no longer felt like an exclusive contract with a large corporate gym franchise was serving their shared vision for intenSati, so they left Equinox. They continued to teach in New York, albeit to smaller classes, and on the road, often selling out big events and retreats. They also started taping online content for YouTube, so they were ready for COVID gym closures in 2020. Osborne told me that within days of the first wave of lockdowns, "we would get four hundred, five hundred, even six hundred people in those classes."

Then the unimaginable happened. Moreno was diagnosed with cervical cancer and got very sick. Some in the intenSati community were so devoted to her and her method that they were convinced she would get better. People would say things like "She's so evolved, how could this happen to her?," and others "spoke as if Patricia should be able to heal herself with the power of her mind alone." But Osborne says that wasn't how Moreno thought about it. She made use of every single therapy available to her, including those offered by conventional Western medicine. Moreno was also no Bryan Johnson. She never promised we could biohack ourselves to health or immortality. As Osborne put it, "She always taught us that life is a co-creation"—we do our part but also depend on other people and "forces in the universe."

In January 2022, Moreno passed away at the age of fifty-seven. As a result, intenSati faced the problem many prophetic religions face: What happens when the charismatic leader dies? In intenSati's case, charisma has been routinized in a couple of ways.

One is the transition to Osborne as the leader of intenSati. Osborne is charismatic, but not quite in the way Moreno was. She has kept the community going after Moreno's death, skillfully curating and holding space for those who continue to mourn Moreno and new members of the community who are just starting their journeys. As the lead teacher of my instenSati instructor training, Osborne was welcoming, patient, warm, and kind. Garside likes to say everyone wanted Moreno to be their mom or lover. Osborne is more like the friend you meet up with for a day in the park or your charming younger sister. If Moreno was a prophet of spiritual fitness, whose charisma came from her physical presence and power, I'd say Osborne's charisma is more about her ability to connect with others.

When Moreno launched her first leader training, Osborne told me, she assumed that it would be mostly for fitness professionals and was frankly surprised that so many non-pros were interested. Today, Osborne is committed to the idea that anyone can teach intenSati. But this poses a new challenge, because it means some potential teachers must develop charisma beyond the physical power or attractiveness of a stereotypical fitness instructor.

I asked Osborne how she thought the teacher training helped with this. She brought up the example of how we begin each class with an introduction unique to the instructor and written for that particular day. According to Osborne, this is one way to create and build trust and connection with students. "Your introduction has to be about what's happening for you right now," Osborne explained. "And you must open up about something, even if it's how annoyed you are that there are dishes in the sink. It doesn't have to be experiencing heartbreak, but it has to be very current for you, and it has to be real."

The first introduction I ever did in my teacher training was for a series called "I Belong." I started off by sharing that one of the affirmations, "I feel grounded today," was challenging for me—especially the "today" part. "I have a lot of trouble living in the moment," I said. "I'm always thinking about tomorrow. I'm thinking about next month. I'm thinking about next year." And then I shared two interactions with my teenager I had had within the last twenty-four hours. In the first, we were scheduling driving lessons and SATs, ping-ponging back and forth without really connecting. But the next was different. We both happened to wander into the kitchen at the same time to have our first cup of coffee, sat, and just talked about boys, what she was enjoying in school, and some family dynamics on a recent visit. We were both present. I ended my introduction by saying, "Let's use today's class to chase that feeling of being present in the moment."

Was any of that profound? Nope. But was it real for me in the moment? Yes. And would sharing it help me connect to students and invite them to be vulnerable as well? Probably. And while that isn't the same as the charisma of someone like Stacey Griffith or Patricia Moreno, it is a form of leadership that establishes trustworthiness and authority.

But it isn't just that charisma within intenSati leadership has transformed. Remember that, according to Weber, a charismatic leader must tap into the needs of a community. And I think the needs of the intenSati community have also changed. In the nineties, the best way to get someone to focus on the "softer" lessons of intenSati, like the power of positive self-talk, was through a hardcore fitness program. But we are now in a different moment. No longer is physical intensity assumed to be the only way transformation can occur. No longer is a low BMI the primary goal of physical movement. Instead, as a culture, we value body positivity and more holistic understandings of fitness. And I think many of us are craving a fitness instructor who is relatable, not just aspirational.

Today, most people who take intenSati do so online. What it might lose in emotional intensity from this format it gains in accessibility and affordability. You can find movement paired with affirmations in a lot of classes these days, but a real community that is truly open to everyone is quite rare. I think it is a big part of intenSati's secret sauce.

I saw how people in that community show up for one another when I watched a recording of a session Osborne hosted a week after Moreno's death. The call begins with Osborne and her wife, Liv, on-screen, dancing to "Higher Love" by Kygo and Whitney Houston, Moreno's favorite song. Then the music is turned down, and Osborne comes closer to the camera and begins speaking as Liv in the background is wiping away tears. "We are here to come together and gather in this space, this place that Moreno gave us," Osborne says, her voice cracking. She takes a deep inhale, her lips quivering. "One of my biggest fears about losing my very best friend was that I would feel so lonely. And I look around and I'm not alone." Tears were streaming down her face.

RESTORING RELIGION TO FITNESS

Like most popular techniques branded as "spiritual," I think spiritual fitness comes with some religious baggage. Going back at least as far as the muscular Christianity movement, physical fitness has been equated with morality. Being unfit has been cast as not only a physical problem but also a moral failing, causing us to feel shame and guilt for never being fit enough. And of course, the fatphobia that runs throughout the fitness industry—which can also be traced to religious ideas of bodily perfection we saw in chapter 4—remains a cause for concern.

But it's helpful to consider how spiritual fitness might help us rethink well-being more generally. What exactly are we searching for in these experiences? Are there reasons we think spiritual exercise techniques can do those things better than other methods of wellness? What assumptions could we interrogate?

Weber's understanding of charisma helps explain what draws folks to spiritual fitness instructors in the first place, and the nature of their power over others. They embody forms of charisma, but they also tap into the existing needs of potential students and clients. It is a two-way street, just like many forms of religious leadership. Religious leaders become popular because they speak to followers in ways that help them solve some problem or understand their lives better. The same is true for fitness gurus.

The concept of charisma inspires some questions we can ask to make sure a particular spiritual fitness program is contributing to our well-being, such as:

- What are you hoping to gain from a spiritual fitness class, and is an exercise instructor the best person to help with that?
- How does a particular instructor embody and express charisma in their classes?
- Is an instructor's charisma aspirational or relatable?
- What sorts of existing needs of potential clients are they tapping into?
- In what ways do spiritual fitness programs routinize charisma beyond a founding fitness celebrity?
- Are there versions of charisma that feel less risky to you and thus more conducive to your well-being?

Your answers to these questions will give you some insight into whether a method is a good fit for you. For example, while

I'm often drawn to aspirational instructors, I have noticed that their versions of embodied fitness come with costs such as unrealistic body goals or overtraining, which leads to injuries. I now seek out different forms of charisma, such as Osborne's more accessible vibe.

Even if the wellness industry still defines health through the psychological lens of individual empowerment, the popularity of spiritual fitness programs points to our yearning for communal experiences as part of well-being. This suggests another set of questions to ask of a fitness program to help us suss out if they have a community that might contribute positively to our well-being:

- What values does a particular community presume or reinforce?
- How accessible is a particular spiritual exercise class?
- Is it affordable to me or others?
- How does accessibility affect whom I will share the space with?
- What is the nature of the community?
- Will that community show up for me outside the studio? Will I show up for it?

Gathering and belonging, whether in a spiritual fitness class or not, can heal us from isolation or a lack of meaning in our lives.

6

Deep Listening

SACRED SOUND'S INSIGHTS INTO THE POWER OF GOOD VIBRATIONS

In March 2024, I fell into a trance in a prewar apartment in Greenwich Village. But at the time, I didn't know that was what happened.

That experience was part of a weekend "gong crawl"—five sound baths in thirty-six hours—that Liz Kineke, a religion journalist who regularly attends sound baths as part of her own spiritual practice, had organized for me to get a sense of New York City's sound-bath subculture. Once something you could only experience in a New Age retreat center—like the Integratron outside Joshua Tree, California—sound baths are gaining popularity as a spiritual wellness practice. Today, sound healing experiences are quite easy to find, if you know where to look, and are part of some spiritual seekers' weekly practice.

To begin our tour, Kineke had arranged for me to experience a session with her favorite gong master, Rev. Laksmi Scalise. On a Saturday evening, I met Kineke at Scalise's apartment just off Sixth Avenue. Scalise greeted us at the door with hugs. Then she led us into her living room, set up with large gongs and dozens of metal singing bowls, where several of her regulars were waiting. I prepared myself as best I could for a vibrational experience, uncertain of what to expect.

Here is what I knew before my first session: During a sound bath, attendees lie down and are "bathed" in vibrations and overtones produced by a practitioner using various instruments. I had heard that the sessions could reduce stress, align chakras, aid spiritual development, and promote general healing. Some claim it's the most effective meditation you will ever do. As Sara Auster, a Brooklyn-based sound therapist, put it, "If meditation is taking the stairs, a sound bath is taking the elevator." Others claim it's the easiest. And to be sure, lying on the ground on pillows, covered with a cozy blanket, with your eyes closed, while someone else unleashes a series of sounds exotic to a Western ear *does* seem a whole lot easier than many of the other wellness activities suggested in my social media feed, such as sitting meditations or extreme diets.

And yet I'm always suspicious when spirituality is presented as a wellness shortcut, which is a key element of sound bath marketing: healing through good vibes, without the work of understanding what that means. I was in Scalise's Greenwich Village apartment to figure out what, if any, deeper religious insight into human well-being sound baths might offer.

A gong and Reiki master whose Instagram bio describes her as an energy worker and astrologer, Scalise is also a minister ordained by the Virginia-based ashram Yogaville. You can experience her sound journeys at the well-known Integral Yoga in the West Village, as well as the more recently opened Official Ritual. However, her most devoted followers prefer the sessions she conducts in her own apartment.

And I could see why immediately. Scalise's apartment was visually chaotic, dark, and layered while also intimate and personal. Every surface was crammed with statues, crystals, and plants in various stages of growth and decay. Couches were pushed to the side to make room for seven mats, her gong collection, and a vast array of metal singing bowls—over fifteen, the largest of which we took turns standing inside while she struck it.

Many of the regulars were themselves "healers," offering various types of bodywork or serving as guides for psychedelic journeys. They chatted about the upcoming solar eclipse, discussed the best place to buy palo santo incense, and complained about the sound of the generator the MTA had set up outside to work on repairs.

Scalise gave me a thick mat to lie on and offered various-sized pillows straight off her couch to try out under my head. Most were leopard print. Then she pointed to a pile of blankets in a cupboard for me to select from.

When it was time to begin, we all lay down and got as cozy as possible. We were separated by only a few inches. If I had wanted to, I could have reached out and held Kineke's hand. I felt everyone around me begin to settle, so I took a breath and closed my eyes.

There wasn't much by way of formal instructions for what we should do. Instead, Scalise spoke to us for a bit about astral journeys and vibrations.

The experience immediately became more intense as soon as Scalise stopped talking and started to coax sounds out of the gongs and metal bowls. Before one gong would stop emitting sound, she'd strike another, so that, very quickly, vibrations seemed to fill the room. It was more percussive than melodic, at least to my untrained ear. I wouldn't describe it as music per se, but it was rich and structured. There was no pattern that I noticed. The only thing that seemed predictable was that the sound was constant.

I understood why this experience is often called a sound bath. I did feel submerged in something viscous, but instead of waves of water, it was waves of sound coming from gongs and metal bowls. We needn't have worried about the generator on the street, because the constant thunder inside completely drowned it out. Frankly, it drowned out everything. The sound became loud and frenetic, ever escalating. I didn't feel dizzy, but I also didn't feel totally in control, almost like I was caught in a rough surf, unable to keep my legs under me.

At the most intense moments, colors swirled behind my closed eyelids—magenta waves, yellow-green and cerulean-blue sparks. I felt specific physical effects, some pleasant, some not. My heart rate slowed. I had a couple of involuntary twitches. A pleasant buzzing started in my right shoulder and spread, at one point, to my lips. About halfway through the session, as I lay on my back, my ankles began to ache so intensely I had to roll onto my side for relief.

Although sound bath advocates refer to the experience as a form of meditation, given my mindfulness experiences (see chapter 2), I don't think *meditation* is the right word. I think Judith Becker, an ethnomusicologist who studies how sound and music facilitate religious experiences, offers a better one: *trance*. She says trancing occurs through sensual overstimulation and involves very strong emotions, a loss of the sense of self, and the breakdown of cognitive thought. That tracks with my experience in Scalise's apartment. If meditation is often practiced in solitude, trancing occurs within a communal framework. If meditation happens through stillness, trancing involves strenuous activity. Most important for this chapter, if meditation happens in silence, trancing is usually accompanied by sound.

I lost track of time in my trancelike state, but after an hour, it was over. I felt emotionally churned up and enormously disoriented, almost stoned. Where had I gone? What caused such intense feelings? I was grateful for the ginger chew Scalise offered from a cut-glass bowl. In the Harry Potter novels, chocolate counteracts an encounter with the dementors. Like that, the ginger was a much-needed antidote.

Scalise seemed to be struggling to stand upright. She declared, "That was a really good one. You all got rid of all kinds of stuff. I could see what you were releasing in the room, on the ceiling." She then confessed, "I had a little trouble speaking at the end. I know I need to speak to bring you out, but sometimes I take a journey too, and it's hard to come back." I nodded, wondering where she had gone and what would have happened to the rest of us if she hadn't returned, as I chewed my ginger candy.

As I tried to transition back into the room, I listened to Scalise and a young attendee discuss how the gong bath reorganized the body's fluids. If we'd had water bottles with us, they agreed, the sound would have reorganized that water as well. I raised an eyebrow at that. Reorganized water? On a molecular level? To be fair, I did feel a bit reorganized. But I was pretty sure it wasn't something the science of fluids could explain.

A handful of scientific studies have tried to measure the effects of sound baths—in terms of decreasing anxiety, not molecular rearrangement. One often-cited 2017 study was led by Tamara Goldsby, a clinical research psychologist who focuses on sound healing as an integrative health technique. That study of sixty-two individuals found that a sound bath of metal and crystal singing bowls, gongs, and small bells in a nonmedical setting—over half of the participants were from the Chopra Center for Wellbeing in Carlsbad, California—decreased patients' anxiety and pain. Jayan Marie Landry, a licensed psychotherapist and registered nurse, published a similar study in 2014 that found singing bowls decreased blood pressure and heart rates in healthy adults in a therapeutic setting.

There are also scientific theories about why sound baths have these effects. Some posit that sound alters brainwave states and that sound baths induce states associated with greater levels of relaxation. Others think the effects of sound baths are the result of the binaural beat phenomenon, which occurs when sounds at two different hertz levels are played, one in each ear, and the brain syncs or "entrains" to the difference between them. And still others suggest that a sound bath stimulates the vagus nerve to produce an increased feeling of well-being. Underlying all these theories is some version of the idea that humans have an internal rhythm that vibrations can alter, thereby improving us.

But science can only tell us so much. It might eventually figure out precisely how specific sounds affect the central nervous system, but that still leaves unanswered the bigger question: What sorts of internal "rhythms" are the most conducive to well-being? The answer to that question depends on what we imagine a fuller life might feel like. For that, we need the help of art, poetry, music, and yes, even religion.

Though the specific sonic elements may vary greatly across religions, understandings of sound are fundamental to religious worldviews. Some religions describe the cosmos as originating from sound. Others use sonic techniques like recitation or chanting to access revelation or as a technique for salvation. In many traditions, certain sounds are believed to have the capacity to purify, to channel divine energies, or to open portals to the sacred realm. In some religious traditions, the divine is portrayed as fundamentally sonic, while for others, sound is a way to access the divine within us. Often the religious experience of sound is communal, as with the African American gospel tradition of call-and-response. Church bells and the Islamic adhan let believers know it is time to gather or pray, and in doing so, create acoustic territories of belonging. Almost every religion has a role for sound in its rituals, from Gregorian chants to Roman Catholic vespers to chanting "om."

Enlightenment intellectuals who privileged our sense of sight and rational abilities might have ignored the role of sound in human flourishing, but religions do not. This chapter tries to recapture some of the religious insights into well-being.

COLLECTIVE EFFERVESCENCE AND SOUND BATHS REVISITED

If we stay with the example of sound baths, you might assume that the way to restore their religion is to understand how they function in their "original" Asian religious and cultural contexts. That was part of how I approached yoga and mindfulness in earlier chapters. But this won't work for sound baths because they're not actually some ancient, sacred practice that we imported from the East. They're something that the spiritual wellness community sort of made up.

Contemporary wellness sound facilitators use several instruments: gongs, crystal bowls, bells, chimes, tuning forks, drums, rainsticks, shruti boxes, and more. But metal bowls, commonly referred to as Tibetan singing bowls, have become the star of Western sound baths—and yet they are not the ancient sacred objects we have been told they are.

While bells and chimes have a history of use in Tibetan religious life, the beloved singing bowl does not. The scholarly consensus is that these bowls were traditionally everyday metal storage bowls, not ritual objects. Their role as sacred objects seems to have begun with the American Nancy Hennings and Henry Wolff's 1972 New Age album, *Tibetan Bells.* Anthropologist Ben Joffe theorizes that Wolf and Hennings applied the principles of Japanese standing bells, which had come to the United States with Zen Buddhist meditation sessions, to the Himalayan metal bowls they saw while visiting Nepal. Tibetan studies scholar Robert Barnett has a different hypothesis. He thinks enterprising Nepali traders might have invented the concept of Tibetan singing bowls in the 1970s to sell everyday storage bowls at a substantial markup to American tourists seeking enlightenment in Tibet's mountains.

Whoever deserves credit for their invention, the metallic bowls that sound healers import for thousands of dollars are not objects used in ancient sacred healing ceremonies. That doesn't mean singing bowls don't work or that they can't have religious significance. It's just that their sacredness isn't rooted in an unbroken Tibetan lineage; it's created by modern practitioners in the West.

Instead of searching for some "original form" of spiritual sound practices like a sound bath—which is frankly a lost cause—a more helpful approach is to look at what purpose sound serves for religious communities and the specific effects of "deep listening," the term Becker uses to describe secular forms of trancing. Religious sound practices and theologies will help us better understand why people are drawn to experiences like sound baths in the first place—and how we can get more out of those experiences, and daily life, by becoming better listeners.

One of the overarching lessons we find from restoring the religious roots of common spiritual wellness practices is that they are more meaningful, responsible, and effective when done in a communal setting. Sound is no different.

I approached my first sound bath experience as a method of personal self-care. But I suspect a community of practice is necessary to access the deeper benefits out of sound. This was made even clearer after my four-year-old nephew, Gus, tried to organize a sound bath for me.

Picture this ridiculous scene. I was visiting Gus and his parents. After thirty minutes of listening to him play his drum kit, desperate for some acoustic relief, I asked him if he might want to give me a sound bath concert. He knew what yoga and meditation were from his progressive preschool, and I explained to him that a sound bath was sort of like that. We would switch off the lights, and he could turn on his Milky Way projector to evoke the feeling of a cosmic journey. Then he could have Alexa play a sound bath while Aunt Liz lay on the floor with her eyes closed.

I thought I was quite clever for coming up with this idea, and I did get to lie down for a few minutes and listen to a recording of crystal bowls and shruti boxes. But there was nothing restorative about Gus's sound bath. In part, that's because hearing a four-year-old shouting orders to Alexa—"No, Alexa, I said play a *smoothing* sound bath!"—is the opposite of relaxing. Gus's significant lack of finesse notwithstanding, it was also not the same to be lying on the floor alone. In Scalise's apartment, I was aware the entire time that I was in a room a few inches from others. I wasn't on the same astral journey as they were, but I knew they were my fellow travelers. It wasn't the same "pretending" with just my nephew. The presence of a community who believed the practice could work mattered.

To help explain why, let's look to Émile Durkheim, the famous French sociologist who understood better than most the importance of a religious community for our well-being. Over a century ago, he described in *The Elementary Forms of Religious Life* how religions provide opportunities for individuals to come together, do something as a group, and enjoy "big feeling" experiences. He thought these intentional, purposeful gatherings were crucial to human well-being, if not our very survival.

According to Durkheim, when we gather with others for a shared purpose and engage in activities together that reaffirm that purpose, we experience *collective effervescence*, a feeling of heightened emotions that are activated and then intensified within the echo chamber of the group. Consider a funeral. Whenever I attend a funeral, even if I didn't know the deceased very well, I find the experience to be emotionally intense because of the collective experience of grieving. Another example of collective effervescence might be a Red Sox game at Fenway Park, which is a particular form of joy for a Bostonian.

Durkheim recognized the important role of sound in creating experiences of collective effervescence—for instance, singing a hymn in a funeral or "Sweet Caroline" in the eighth-inning stretch at Fenway Park. A result of "emitting same cries, words and gestures," according to Durkheim, is that "participants nourish the group feeling." And so we have a mutual feedback loop. We gather as a group, participate in shared activities that reinforce a sense of belonging, and therefore want to gather again. That is how a community is formed.

When I think back on my gong crawl, I see that when the sound experiences required participation of some sort from the group, my emotional response intensified, often tenfold. This was especially true at my last sound bath experience that weekend in an unlikely location: an Episcopal church.

All Saints' Episcopal Church in Brooklyn offers a sound-bath-infused service most Sunday evenings, building on the Anglican tradition of Evensong, a combination of hymns, scriptural readings, and prayers near sunset. In addition to a choir, a priest, and a few altar servers, a sound facilitator by the name of Alex Beckmann helps lead this sound-based liturgy.

This mash-up is the brainchild of the Reverend Steven Paulikas, rector at All Saints', who thought those drawn to sound baths might also experience the church's liturgy as powerful. He decided that offering a service with both elements would be one way to make that possible.

When I attended All Saints' Evensong, it at first felt odd to enter such a Christian space for a sound bath, which is neither traditional to nor associated with Christianity. Beckmann had set up in the center of the altar with his shruti box, gong, and singing bowls. A group of about forty of us settled in the pews. Then the priest, choir, and altar servers entered and began a forty-five-minute service that combined the vibrations of a sound bath with biblical readings and choir music, all while the setting sun streamed through stained glass windows.

For me, the most powerful part of the service was the group vocalization at the end. Beckmann led us in a series of oms at different pitches. The om vibrated in my chest, and hearing the collective om made my skin tingle. It made me feel connected, part of a congregation, in a way the other liturgical elements had not. It showed me sound could be recruited to foster belonging, not just diminish an individual's stress.

But I knew there was more that religions can teach us about sound. For instance, Kineke had an experience in Scalise's apartment that was very different from mine, and not only because she was part of that group of regulars. She was also skilled in listening in a particular way. In "spiritual but not religious" sound experiences like a sound bath, newbies like me are often left to try to figure out the experience's meaning alone. Without some instruction, I didn't know how to make sense of it.

But that's the point, you might be thinking. *Everyone can take from sound bath what they want.* Self-service is the first rule of the spiritual salad bar. And the idea that sound baths are "easy," requiring no expertise and very little effort from the participant, is incredibly widespread, even in supposedly unbiased scientific studies. For instance, an often-cited 2017 paper found that sound bath newcomers reported a slightly larger effect than those who had attended sound baths before and concluded that "sound healing has no learning curve for participants."

But I want to suggest an alternative. Maybe it's not that experience is irrelevant to sound bath efficacy but rather that merely attending more sound baths doesn't necessarily teach us how to get more out of each one. Maybe for that we need something like an Evensong liturgy or a sacred text or an intentional community that teaches us to listen more instead of less to the soundscapes around us. Maybe we need a different sort of training, one that exposes us to religious understandings of sound.

What might that training look like? It would depend on what a particular community of practice emphasized. I took a look at two very different ones—Sikh kirtan and Islamic cassette sermons—to understand the different ways religious communities train their members to be better listeners.

THE EMOTIONAL INTELLIGENCE OF SIKH KIRTAN

We all have experiences with how sound can affect our moods. A workout playlist to amp us up. Classical music to wind down at the end of the day. A mixtape to process our sadness after a breakup. Religious communities can help us think more deeply about the role of these sound-evoked emotions in our well-being, as well as about how we might learn to listen in ways that invite emotional intensity.

One religious example I found helpful on this topic is kirtan, a form of devotional chanting accompanied by instruments like the harmonium, sitar, tabla, rabaab, and tambourine. Originating in India, kirtan gained visibility in the West in the 1960s through new religious movements like the International Society for Krishna Consciousness (ISKCON) and Yogananda's Self-Realization Fellowship. While those forms of kirtan were devotional, they inspired looser spiritual forms of kirtan that have become increasingly popular among spiritual seekers and are offered in yoga studios, wellness retreat centers, and music festivals. Like yoga, there are spiritual forms of kirtan as well as more religious ones.

Some Western spiritual kirtan performers have achieved superstar status. Krishna Das and Jai Uttal, for instance, are both Grammy-nominated white Western men trained partially in India. They perform at sold-out kirtan concerts for those seeking an ecstatic experience of big feelings like bliss and euphoria.

I attended a Krishna Das concert by chance in 2019 while completing my yoga teacher training at the Kripalu retreat center in the Berkshires. In general, concerts are not my thing. They're too loud. When my fellow yoga teacher trainee told me ecstatic dancing was a big part of the experience, I was even more apprehensive. But I was curious what all the fuss was about, so I agreed to go.

I arrived late and was handed a printout of some lyrics. Krishna Das was seated at the front of the hall on a slightly raised stage, accompanied by five other musicians. He was singing and playing a harmonium, an organ-like instrument that uses bellows to create a melody. The other musicians were playing hand drums, a violin, and other stringed and percussion instruments. Kirtan concerts follow a progressively more intense arc, and by the time I entered the great hall, the place was whipped into a frenzy. Attendees were either spinning around with their eyes closed and their hands in the air or they were rocking in their seats. Most were singing along, chanting the last line of "Baba Hanuman," a spiritual song by Krishna Das: "Hare Raama Raama Raama, Seetaa Raama Raama Raama." The chant was catchy, and Krishna Das's deep voice was lovely, but the chaotic energy overwhelmed me. I left after ten minutes.

Much of the Western kirtan scene that Krishna Das is part of is presented as spiritual but detached from specific religious traditions. It is an item on the spiritual wellness salad bar available to all, including the spiritual but not religious. Might there be something to learn about the role of sound in well-being from more explicitly religious forms of kirtan? Hindu, Sufi, and Sikh traditions all practice it. Let's consider the Sikh version.

Singing and listening to liturgical chants are central to Sikh worship. The founder of Sikhism, Guru Nanak, and his nine successors communicated with worshippers primarily through song. The Sikh primary sacred text, Siri Guru Granth Sahib, is a songbook. Sikh devotional music, known as Gurbani kirtan, has become increasingly important to American Sikhs since the 1980s as part of efforts to keep a new generation connected to their traditions and history. We can say that Gurbani kirtan is a way to access both Sikh wisdom and Sikh ethics. Its specific religious content, like the embodied values of yoga, is not coincidental. It is the point.

Getting the full benefits of Gurbani kirtan requires learning to listen differently, or as the Sikh musician Bhai Gurcharan Singh says, it requires one to "improve upon their taste of the ears." If we listen in an ordinary or uneducated way, as I did when attending Krishna Das's concert, there might be some benefits, but they are only partial.

So how can we listen more like Sikhs? Or, to put it a bit more generally, how can we refine our listening so that we "taste" much more? To learn more, I enrolled in a mini-course offered by Raj Academy, an organization established in 1994 that works to educate the public on "the science of sound from Sikh Music to heal the mind."

The course began by explaining that sound is important in the Sikh tradition because it enables worshippers to connect with what cannot be expressed in words, such as emotions, which are central to human life. "We are 'feeling' beings," Raj Academy teaches. "Simply by knowing our feelings, we can change the course of our life." Specific sonic experiences, like kirtan, can train us how to acknowledge what we are feeling, and then help us to express those emotions. Doing so, Sikhs believe, can be personally healing. It is also a way to increase our emotional intelligence. Through sensory awareness we are better able to recognize and understand the emotions of others.

During the course, I learned that the canonical Sikh text Siri Guru Granth Sahib is organized by different musical moods known as raags—sixty raags in all. For instance, "Raag Aasaa" is associated with inspiration, courage, and motivation, "Raag Gauri Deepaki" with comfort and security, "Raag Majh" with extreme love but also the sorrow of separation, and "Raag Gauri Chayti" with feelings of panic and regret. The text teaches that all these moods are valuable—not just feelings of positivity or bliss.

Let me pause here for a moment, because I think this is a profound insight. We seem to be in a particular cultural moment when we equate mental health with feeling good and are uneasy with any challenging or uncomfortable emotions. But intense sonic experiences don't always generate positive feelings; they can be profoundly unsettling as well. The Sikh tradition of kirtan encourages followers to explore the full range of human emotions—joy, yes, but also sorrow, regret, and panic—to help us gain greater insight into ourselves and the world around us. Feeling all the feelings in this worldview, not just the pleasant ones, is what real well-being looks like.

Intense sonic experiences don't always generate positive feelings; they can be profoundly unsettling as well. Kirtan encourages followers to explore the full range of human emotions.

The kirtan course included prompts for how to foster the skills necessary for more intentional listening. We were told to note how we felt after experiencing a few minutes of kirtan. We were encouraged to "breathe in" those emotions and try to remember what really feeling those big feelings is like. We were asked to consider how we might apply kirtan-prompted moods to our life more generally.

Sikhs say these listening skills can have devotional benefits, such as an improved connection with the divine creators. But they also believe deep listening can have social benefits. As the educational nonprofit SikhNet puts it,

> *Active listening is something that requires energy and focus. It's a skill that's needed in every aspect of life; from family and work, to volunteerism and leadership. Kirtan teaches us how to listen actively. . . . Think of the many conflicts that happen either at home or in the workplace. How many of these situations were a result of someone not listening or properly understanding a particular point? We all want to be listened to and understood.*

The portable idea here is that deep listening doesn't only affect the individual. It can also strengthen their connections to others.

ISLAMIC CASSETTE SERMONS AND MORAL DISCERNMENT

If you've made it this far into the book, you've probably figured out that I'm interested in how restoring religious context to wellness practices can make them more ethical. And in fact, Émile Durkheim thought collective effervescence did more than just reinforce the group. He thought those big feelings led to a "moral remaking" in which shared sentiments of the group are not only reaffirmed but sometimes discovered and imprinted on us. If he was right, group sound practices have the potential to change who we are.

In his book *The Ethical Soundscape*, anthropologist Charles Hirschkind takes a deep dive into the role of Islamic cassette sermons in Egypt to describe how this community morally remakes itself through sound. Cassette sermons, and Islamic ones at that, probably don't immediately come to mind as a method of achieving well-being. Non-Muslims, if they've heard of them at all, are more likely to associate them with religious militancy than with right living ever since Ayatollah Khomeini used them to help mobilize Iranian Muslims for the 1979 Revolution. However, Hirschkind finds that cassette sermons in Cairo focus on personal piety, not political militancy. And, important for our purposes, their widespread use cultivates specific types of listening skills within that Muslim community.

During his time in Cairo in the 1990s, Hirschkind found that cassette-recorded sermons by popular Islamic preachers were sold everywhere (at mosques, on the street, in bookstores, in bus stations) and played everywhere (in homes, in taxis, in cafés). They are a major component of what he calls the local ethical soundscape.

What makes this soundscape ethical? you might ask. It is true that cassette sermons function partly as entertainment. Much as I put on a podcast while I'm cooking dinner, Egyptians might play cassette sermons in the background while working or performing mundane tasks. For this purpose, listening skills can be quite basic. But entertainment is not the only goal of cassette sermons, and it is certainly not the highest religious goal.

Arabic has two words for listening: *samʿ*, merely hearing, or, *al-insat*, listening with attention. The first happens spontaneously without much effort on our part, as when I half listen to a podcast while cooking. But listening with attention, which Egyptians describe as "listening with the heart," is an active, not passive, activity. It requires training, skills, and some degree of follow-through. For example, listening with attention to a sermon entails not only understanding its content but also applying the lessons learned from the sermon to one's life. That last aspect is important—to listen well requires a change in behavior. Preaching instructor Muhammad Subhi acknowledges that sound can bring comfort, "a kind of catharsis," but cautions, "Things must not stop at this feeling." Instead, to be truly effective, listening "must be transformed into part of one's practical reality."

Hirschkind argues that sensitive Muslim listeners are more likely to behave morally because they are also skilled at what ethicists call *moral discernment.* Moral discernment involves understanding the ethical issues at stake in any given course of action, the positions or interests of others, and the possible effects our actions might have on both us and those around us. It enables us to determine which action might best contribute to our specific goals, whether that be living according to God's will or contributing to social justice. It requires being perceptive and receptive before responding to any situation.

What Hirschkind learned is that for the Muslim community he studied, moral discernment is not just a rational or cognitive process. It depends on a "moral physiology, the affective-kinesthetic experience of a body permeated by faith" that can occur when listening to a sermon.

What is the takeaway from this study of cassette sermons for those of us who aren't Muslim? It suggests that active listening during sound baths and other forms of sonic wellness practices might be opportunities for ethical training. That both encourages us to reflect on how we're listening and seek out ways to get better at listening. Deep listening as discernment is a life skill that allows us to understand the world around us well enough to act in ways that are consistent with our values.

RESTORING RELIGION TO SOUND

Judith Becker, author of *Deep Listeners*, argues that deep listening is a "life-enhancing, personally enriching skill." If true, it is a skill I lack. I have never been taught that deep listening is important, or how I might do it. I rarely consider sound's positive contribution to my well-being—quite the opposite, in fact. I sleep and work with earplugs. I walk the dog wearing noise-canceling headphones. I'm a curator of silence. Why?

Music historian Ted Gioia offers an answer. In his book *Healing Songs*, he suggests that we used to be better listeners but today we work harder to block out sounds than we do to truly hear them. We screen out traffic, flyovers, whining kids, the hum of the HVAC, and the buzz of our electronic gadgets. But in these attempts to manage the noise pollution of modern life, we forget that listening deeply is part of being fully human.

Alexandre Tannous, an ethnomusicologist and prominent sound therapist, says that the purpose of sound is "not to teach us anything new, but to help us remember, to reclaim, something very, very old." What is reclaimed is both simple and radical. It is the insistence that our well-being depends on careful attention to the world around us, which requires honing all our senses, including our hearing.

Religious practices of sound have some insight on how to do this. They offer ways to understand a deeper purpose for sound. In religious contexts, sound is framed as creating intense collective experiences and forming group bonds. It can encourage us to feel a wide range of emotions, which in turn makes us more emotionally intelligent. And listening, done well within a religious community of support, can morally remake us. For instance, kirtan is part of how the Sikh community instills its values in community members.

Many religions see deep listening as an ethical practice furthering communal moral goals. We have seen that Islamic cassette sermons draw on the idea that if we take the time to learn to listen "with our heart," we'll be able to discern reality more fully. We then become more likely to act morally, because we can better decipher the ethical stakes of any situation we find ourselves in. Sound experiences in this framing are not just opportunities to unwind but also opportunities to gain the skills necessary to live lives consistent with our core values. Once we acknowledge that sonic effects can be morally meaningful and lasting, we can articulate for ourselves what values we might want to remember or enact during a specific sound experience.

These insights into sound all rest on two assumptions about human nature: that we are sensory beings, and that we are fundamentally relational. True well-being requires more than a personal pursuit of chasing good vibes. To be fully human, we need to experience all the vibes. And we need to do this with others.

True well-being requires more than chasing good vibes. To be fully human, we need to experience all the vibes.

Let's go back to Scalise's apartment and consider how what we have learned might help make sense out of what I did, and did not, experience that day.

I was a newbie to sound baths before my New York City gong crawl. I had expected a relaxing, meditative experience. What I got felt more like a taste of frenetic trancing. My conclusion after that weekend? Sound baths are powerful. However, while those first experiences were intense, they were temporary. I think that was because I didn't really understand the importance of why and how sound matters for our well-being.

First, I was completely unprepared for the experience. I lacked the training necessary for fully engaging with sound. I hadn't read a sacred text, participated in sound-rich environments where deep listening was a practiced skill, or grown up in a community that regularly engaged in intense sonic rituals. It was all new to me. And so of course I was a bad listener.

Second, I mistakenly assumed that a sound bath was solely a passive and relaxing activity. I didn't know that I, too, played an active role, and I was unaware of the nature of that role. When the gongs intensified and I felt overwhelmed, I lacked the skills to fully embrace this emotional sensory arousal. Furthermore, I hadn't considered how to integrate this experience into the rest of my day.

Third, I hadn't realized how important a community of listeners would be to my own sonic experiences. There was a group present at Scalise's apartment who shared the conviction that we were embarking on cosmic journey. But I didn't feel part of it, and that is why her sound bath left me so disoriented. In contrast, I did feel a part of the group of people who showed up at All Saints' Evensong—I think because that entire group felt sort of random, like a room full of first-timers, and I became pretty emotional when we chanted "om" as a congregation. Much of spiritual seeking is motivated by feelings of isolation and loneliness, so it's helpful to realize that communal sound experience can foster a sense of belonging and form a real community.

My next sound bath will be different. I'll expect trancing instead of meditation. I'll consider what community I might be joining. I'll practice deep listening, focusing intently on overtones and their interplay. I'll welcome a full spectrum of emotions, both positive and negative. And I will consciously apply the insights gained to my daily life, aiming for a deeper, more empathetic engagement with the world around me and the people in it. For me, the next sound bath will be less about escaping the stresses of the workweek and more about developing the skills needed to navigate challenging interactions with my four-year-old nephew.

7

Psychedelic Sacraments

MIND-ALTERING TRIPS FOR HEALING AND LEARNING TO DIE

In September 2024, I spent three days in a yurt in southern Oregon with forty other people, dressed in white, singing Portuguese-language hymns and channeling spirits as part of a ceremony organized by the Santo Daime Church of the Holy Light of the Queen. It was the hardest three days of research I have ever done, and the fact that I was tripping on ayahuasca the entire time was the least of it.

Investigating this particular wellness practice posed a challenge for me, because before starting this research, I had never tried psychedelics and never really wanted to. I grew up during the war on drugs and was an early convert to Nancy Reagan's

"Just say no" campaign. Plus, I'm a rule follower, and psychedelics are legally classified as Schedule I drugs, which groups them with heroin.

But a book about popular spiritual wellness practices must include psychedelics. No longer taboo, both natural and synthetic psychoactive substances have become popular additions to wellness regimes—microdosing mushrooms to take the edge off a hard day, using LSD to rewire your mind, taking MDMA to lighten the mood, and attending ayahuasca retreats for self-transformation. Studies out of universities like Johns Hopkins, Columbia, and the University of Texas have found psychedelics effective in treating substance abuse, anxiety, postpartum depression, and PTSD. Some of these trials reported life-changing effects in deeply religious terms, and others tried to measure mystical experience.

My hunch was that religious communities with histories of psychedelic use have ways of thinking about them that are missing from their current recreational and therapeutic exploration. For instance, psychedelics are powerful but also potentially dangerous. *How do religious communities mitigate that risk?* A lot of people approach psychedelics as shortcuts, substances that can create a peak experience that will change our lives. *But if those experiences don't orient us in the days that follow, aren't we missing their true power? What frameworks do religions have to prevent psychedelic epiphanies from fading?* I was sure that, as with so many other popular forms of spiritual wellness practices, we could better understand psychedelics by taking religious histories, doctrines, and rituals more seriously.

My initial plan was to explore this topic at arm's length. I would interview others about their experiences with psychedelics, good and bad, and see if religion could help make some sense of what was happening. My rationale was that you don't have to partake in sound baths to integrate religious lessons about deep listening, be recovering from addiction to integrate AA's idea that we are not-God into your life, or attend a spiritual fitness class to understand the power of collective effervescence. Certainly, the same could be said of psychedelics. There must be insights into consciousness or the spiritual realm that I could glean without actually getting high.

But a series of events in 2024 convinced me otherwise.

First, I had lunch in late summer with Don Lattin in Oakland, California. Don is no stranger to psychedelics or religion. A journalist and author, he has written several books on the topic, including the national bestseller *The Harvard Psychedelic Club* and most recently *God on Psychedelics.*

Over bowls of handmade pasta, I came to realize Don and I don't approach the topic of religion and psychedelics with the same goal. For Don, the magic of psychedelics is they can help us restore aspects of religion that have too often been forgotten—like mystery, awe, and transcendence—without all the baggage of dogma and doctrine. In contrast, I wonder how some of that dogma and doctrine might help psychedelics work better for us. In other words, my question was something like: *So you like to trip on mind-altering plants . . . could the experience be "more" with religion in the room?* I was hoping Don would help me decide which psychedelic religious community to focus on. Frankly, I was overwhelmed by all the options.

Many of us associate plant psychedelics with Native communities, but for good reasons, those communities do not like to invite outsiders into their religious ceremonies. There is a very well-known case of white Americans "ruining the medicine" for the Mexican village of Huautla. After a 1957 *Life* magazine article in which Gordon Wasson, a J.P. Morgan banker turned psychedelic enthusiast, described the use of psilocybin mushrooms there, the town was inundated with spiritual seekers, and the local healer—Maria Sabina—was eventually shunned by her community. This story is a cautionary tale for researchers and psychedelic advocates alike.

There are two well-known religious psychedelic organizations, Ligare and Shefa, that help Christians and Jews respectively process and integrate psychedelic experiences. I told Don I was considering interviewing their members, but he had a different opinion of what I should do: focus on the Brazilian-based Santo Daime church, which consumes ayahuasca as a sacrament.

Ayahuasca is a brew made from cooking the stems of the *Banisteriopsis caapi* vine and the leaves of the *Psychotria viridis* shrub, which contains the psychoactive compound dimethyltryptamine, or DMT. Recreational use is illegal in the United States, Canada, and most European countries, but over the last decade it has become trendy to travel to wellness retreats in places including Ecuador, Peru, Costa Rica, and Brazil to participate in ayahuasca ceremonies. Some go seeking "healing," either from emotional trauma or illness. Others hope to experience the trip that "the mother of psychedelics" has to offer.

These retreat centers weren't attractive sites for my research. First, I wasn't sure how much religion I'd find. Ayahuasca does have a tradition of ritualized use by Indigenous Amazonian communities, but that is not what these retreat centers are. To be sure, they claim to offer an ancient Indigenous ceremony and are often led by someone who calls themselves a shaman, but they are for-profit centers catering to tourists willing to pay thousands of dollars for a life-transforming experience. Traditional spiritual healers have accused these centers of exploiting Indigenous peoples and their knowledge traditions. As Diana Negrín, a geographer with expertise in Indigenous studies, points out, "The global consumption of these plants reflects relations of power rooted in the racial order created with colonialism and the ongoing destruction of the very habitat these plants are endemic to." This means "seemingly benign practices aimed at therapy or recreation are endangering the very plants they are celebrating."

Second, many retreat centers are shrouded in scandals and controversies. Shamans who are con artists, cases of sexual assault and rape of female attendees, and even murder—these have all been exposed by journalists. I wanted to study psychedelic use in a religious community in part because I thought religion could create a safe container. I didn't trust that a retreat center would offer that.

Not to mention ayahuasca is considered by many to be the most intense of the psychedelics currently for offer on the spiritual salad bar. Not exactly ideal for a newbie like me.

And so when Don suggested I look into an ayahuasca church, I said, "Jeez, Don, that is not what I want."

"No, it is exactly what you want," he insisted. "Those folks are really serious about their religion." And a 2006 Supreme Court decision meant a handful of ayahuasca churches in the United States can legally import their tea from Brazil, so I would avoid breaking any laws.

"But ayahuasca?" I protested. "Everyone says that's the most intense one!"

"You could just go and microdose a bit, and that would be pretty safe."

I left my conversation with Don intrigued to learn more about the Santo Daime religion. For a religious studies nerd like me, this relatively new religion is fascinating. Its founder, Raimundo Irineu Serra, was born in Brazil in 1890 and drank ayahuasca for the first time in the Amazon around 1914. The first official Santo Daime ritual, known as a *trabalho,* or "work," took place in Rio Branco, Brazil, in 1930.

Santo Daime is a syncretic or hybrid religion, a mash-up of several existing religious beliefs and practices, which is something that often happens when different religious traditions come into close contact with one another. Given the history and ethnic makeup of Brazil, Santo Daime has aspects of Catholicism, West African religion, spiritualism, and Indigenous ceremony. There is lots of Jesus talk, a double cross is a central symbol, many of the prayers (like the Lord's Prayer) are virtually identical to Catholic versions, but the hymns are received through revelation in Portuguese. Mediumship—yes, I mean the actual channeling of spirit beings—enters Santo Daime through the integration of members of the Brazilian Umbanda community, and it is a central part of their ceremonies.

And most importantly, instead of the Eucharist of wafer and wine, the holy ayahuasca tea—which they call Daime—is consumed. Daime, which in Portuguese means "give me," is a vehicle for direct communion with the divine but is also considered to be the embodied divine sprit. Much the same way the Catholic Church believes in the doctrine of transubstantiation, Daimists believe that in the process of combining and cooking the vine and leaves of two plants, the Daime tea becomes "ensouled" with the divine.

As part of my research, I read William Barnard's *Liquid Light: Ayahuasca Spirituality and the Santo Daime Tradition* and Ernesto Londoño's *Trippy: The Peril and Promise of Medicinal Psychedelics.* Both tell the story of their experience taking the Daime under the guidance of Jonathan Goldman, who cofounded the Church of the Holy Light of the Queen in Ashland, Oregon, with his wife, Jane Seligson. Barnard and Londoño describe their own visions during the Daime ceremony as well as forms of spirit channeling and mediumship they witnessed. It sounded like just what I was looking for. I emailed Jonathan, and a few weeks later we connected over Zoom.

My plan was to convince him I was not out to expose or embarrass his community but to get his permission to observe a Daime ceremony. I thought I could just take some notes about the hymns, the liturgy, the symbols in the room, and so forth, and that would help me describe how a religious container was important to the safety and efficacy of the Daime. But the call didn't go the way I expected.

Jonathan and I realized we were both in Brazil in the late 1980s, me living with my family in Rio, Jonathan having his first experience with Santo Daime. He asked if I still spoke Portuguese, which I sadly don't, at least not well, but I still understand it a bit. And I love the way it sounds. I explained more about the book I was writing and what I was trying to learn about Santo Daime. Jonathan said I should come out that winter to participate in one of their self-transformation ceremonies and then a more formal set of trabalhos at the church. If I timed it correctly, I could also meet several Brazilians who would be visiting. At this point, nothing had been said about me ingesting anything.

Then, somehow, it came up that one space had just opened in a ceremony at the end of the month—the same weekend I'd just had to cancel a different research trip. Jonathan laughed when I told him that and said I was being "set up." That made me giggle nervously. Then his tone became serious. "I think you should come this month, and drink the Daime with us," he said. "It's the only way to get the answers to the types of questions you're asking." Too many things were aligning, he said, for me not to come.

Ten days after that call, I was sitting in a yurt with ayahuasca in my system.

A BRIEF HISTORY OF RELIGION AND PSYCHEDELICS

The earliest written record we have of the religious use of plant psychedelics is in the Vedas, a collection of Hindu sacred texts codified as early as 1500 BCE. The Rig Veda contains 120 hymns about a plant called *soma.* When priests ingested it, they were said to travel to new worlds, have face-to-face encounters with gods, and even attain immorality. Some modern scholars think soma was a mushroom; others think it was cannabis. No matter what it was, it clearly had a central role in Vedic practice.

A similar psychoactive elixir, *amrita*, is found in Vajrayana Buddhist scriptures from the fifth and sixth centuries and was used in initiations and Tantric feasts. Mike Crowley, a psychedelically inclined Buddhist and author of the book *Secret Drugs of Buddhism*, explains amrita was consumed "to remove the belief in the personal ego and to dissolve the boundary between the guru and the student undergoing the initiation." A nonpsychotropic recipe is still used in Vajrayana rituals today.

Ancient Greeks also experimented with psychedelics, most famously in the Eleusinian Mysteries, which were celebrated for over a thousand years. The Mysteries began as a local ritual in the Greek city of Eleusis but spread during the Roman Empire. The celebration took place over four days, climaxing in a ritual so secret that participants vowed never to share the details on pain of death.

Nevertheless, we do have some reports of what took place during these ceremonies. Apparently, during the final secret rite, initiates consumed a sacred potion, the *kykeon*, that revealed the "Great Mystery" to them. The ancient Greek lyric poet Pindar wrote that someone who has seen the rites "knows the end of life, as well as its divinely granted beginning." The famous Roman philosopher Cicero referred to the Mysteries as "sublime" and credited them with making it possible to "not only live more joyfully but also die with a better hope."

Given the visionary state the kykeon produced, several scholars have posited that it had some psychedelic property. The authors of the book *The Road to Eleusis* (which include Albert Hofmann, the chemist who discovered LSD) suggest kykeon contained LSD-like compounds found in ergot fungus, common in wild grass in the Mediterranean. The active ingredient could also have been psilocybin from local mushrooms, opium from poppies, or DMT from local plants.

If our knowledge of ancient religious use of psychedelics is a bit speculative, modern Indigenous use is not. We have several examples of ceremonial use of plant psychedelics including psilocybin mushrooms, mescaline cactus (peyote), and the DMT plant combo (ayahuasca) in Native communities. Scholars have traced the ceremonial use of mind-altering plants back to the Aztecs and Incas, who used them to cause visions, cure physical or mental illness, or resolve disputes.

Natalie Avalos, a scholar of Indigenous religion, explained to me that key to understanding Native use of plant psychedelics is that the plants are seen as kin. She means this literally. They have personhood, consciousness, and agency in Indigenous worldviews. This means they are not a commodity that should be owned, marketed, or sold. Plant psychedelics are our relatives. They are teachers insofar as they have wisdom to share with us, and we have a responsibility to use any knowledge we receive from them for the collective good. Put differently, the Native understanding of the healing of plant medicine is that it is not just for the individual. It should benefit the land, plants, animals, and broader human community. If we forget that, we're essentially disrespecting the plant medicine, and it can decide to not work for us, because it has agency too.

Plant psychedelics have personhood, consciousness, and agency in Indigenous worldviews. They are not a commodity that should be owned, marketed, or sold.

The Native American Church (NAC), which uses peyote ritually as a sacrament, plays an important role in the history of the legalization of the religious use of psychedelics in the United States. This church combines elements of Christianity and traditional tribal beliefs. It is monotheistic, teaching that there is one Great Spirit, but also has a role for lesser spirits. Jesus is an important figure for the NAC, but so are tribal ancestors. The church integrates the Ten Commandments but interprets them through traditional Native values.

The particular religious mash-up of the NAC makes sense if we consider some pressures on Native Americans during the late nineteenth and early twentieth centuries. Missionaries were actively attempting to convert Indigenous populations to Christianity. Boarding schools separated Native children from their families and forced them to abandon their traditional languages and customs and adopt Christian names and practices. The Dawes Act of 1887 divided tribal lands into individual plots and undermined communal landownership. The westward expansion of white settlers meant the loss of sacred sites and the forced relocations of Native populations to reservations. Traditional Indigenous ceremonies and practices were outlawed or heavily discouraged by the government. And this paragraph is only scratching the surface.

One response to these threats was the Ghost Dance movement. This intertribal movement used a ritual based on a traditional "round dance" to reunite with dead ancestors who could help return peace and prosperity to the Native American peoples. Communities regularly gathered to perform Ghost Dance ceremonies, which made it easier for tribes to share practices. It was in this climate of religious revival and new intertribal cooperation that peyote, common in healing ceremonies of Indigenous groups in Mexico, became more common in the United States, where it had rarely been used before the 1890s.

Native communities who use peyote do so not merely for the mind-altering experiences it offers. They believe the plant can heal physical and spiritual ailments, including addiction. Peyote is also seen as a teacher of ethical ways of living, imparting essential values such as hard work, humility, familial responsibility, loyalty, and the avoidance of anger, gambling, and alcohol.

But peyote's legal status was tricky. Anti-peyote legislation, such as the Hayden Bill of 1918, attempted to ban its use, but First Amendment protections of the free exercise of religion provided an avenue for legality—if Native communities could prove peyote was part of their religious practice. And so in 1918 the Native American Church of North America was incorporated in Oklahoma to gain legal protection for the sacramental use of peyote.

In some ways, the NAC was an attempt to resurrect Native ceremonies while also embracing elements of Christianity reimagined for Native goals. It was likely successful in achieving legal recognition for its sacramental use of a plant psychedelic at least partially because its Christian elements helped the American legal system read it as a religion—unlike in the *Sedlock v. Baird* case from chapter 1, which ruled that wellness yoga was not religious because it didn't comport with Protestant notions of religion as belief. Santo Daime is quite similar to NAC—a mash-up of Christianity and Indigenous religion—and the Religious Freedom Restoration Act is what allowed churches like Jonathan Goldman's Church of the Holy Light of the Queen to argue successfully they have a legal right to use ayahuasca in their religious services.

THE GOOD FRIDAY EXPERIMENT

Twentieth-century use of plant psychedelics was not limited to Native communities or new religious movements that drew from their ceremonies. Others wanted in on this experience as well, and psychedelic experimentation ramped up in the mid-twentieth century when they were still legal. Some advocates of psychedelics suggested they could be shortcuts to the sorts of life-changing supernatural experiences that religious mystics dedicate their lives to achieving. Rather than study, devotion, or ascetic practices, all that was needed was the courage to ingest a mind-altering substance.

Based on his own experience with psilocybin in Mexico, clinical psychologist Timothy Leary organized the Psilocybin Project at Harvard. Leary knew psychology, microbiology, and chemistry could offer only a partial explanation of the power of psychedelics. For a full picture, he would also need religion.

One of the most famous experiments to emerge from that project was the 1962 Good Friday Experiment. Designed by Walter Pahnke as part of his doctoral research at Harvard's Divinity School, its goal was to test whether psilocybin could facilitate a mystical experience if consumed in a religious setting by a group of religiously identifying participants. He gathered twenty volunteers, mostly students from Andover Newton Theological School, along with ten guides, in the basement of Boston University's Marsh Chapel. Half the volunteers and guides received psilocybin, the other half a placebo of nicotinic acid. The service, which included a sermon by Howard Thurman, who inspired the work of Martin Luther King, was broadcast into the basement on speakers.

In the basement that day was a man named Huston Smith. Smith was born into a family of Protestant missionaries in China, but he was more interested in teaching than evangelizing and returned to the United States for college and then graduate school at the University of Chicago. Smith developed a deep interest in mysticism that led him to become involved in Leary's psychedelic research group while he was teaching at MIT. For Smith, the key question was, *Could plant-based medicines and new wonder drugs facilitate true mystical experiences?*

As a result of his participation in the Good Friday Experiment, Smith concluded the answer was yes. He wrote, "For as long as I can remember I have believed in God. . . . But until the Good Friday Experiment, I had had no direct personal encounter with God of the sort that *bhakti yogis*, Pentecostals, and born-again Christians describe. The Good Friday Experiment changed that."

But Smith also had concerns. In a 1964 essay titled "Do Drugs Have Religious Import?," he argued that psychedelics can induce what he would call a religious experience—like his personal experience in the Good Friday Experiment—but he cautioned that "it is less evident that they can produce religious lives." What Smith meant is that the intensity of a psychedelic experience lacks staying power, and there was no guarantee people would emerge better—more moral, more caring, better members of society—from it. In fact, he eventually broke from Leary's group over concerns that the community he was building was hedonistic, selfish, and immoral. Smith thought religion could help by showing how the psychedelic experience put demands on our life going forward, such as changing how we treat others or contribute to the collective good.

MY DAIME TRIP IN THREE ACTS

I was thinking of Huston Smith when I traveled to Ashland, Oregon, for my Santo Daime ceremony at Jonathan Goldman and Jane Seligson's Church of the Holy Light of the Queen.

What would the religious setting or "container" add to the psychedelic encounter, especially for someone like me who's terrified of the hallucinogenic trip? Would it help me feel safe? Would it provide concepts to help interpret what happened? Would it help the experience seem more "real"? And would it affect how I lived my life after?

With those questions in mind, I present to you my Daime trip in three acts.

Act 1: Meeting the Cast of Characters

On the first morning, I woke up, ironed an all-white linen outfit, and made my way to the lobby of my hotel to meet Juan, who had offered me a ride to the Church of the Holy Light of the Queen. Juan asked what had brought me to the ceremony, and when I told him about my research, he said, "You're really going to walk the dog." Director of a palliative care team at a major hospital, he had originally come to Santo Daime out of an interest in how psychedelics could help patients decide if they wanted physician-assisted death. He was not a Santo Daime initiate but had been to several ceremonies.

The location of the ceremony was the Goldman-Seligson property, a thinly wooded plot on a hillside about twenty minutes outside downtown Ashland. After a bumpy drive up a dirt driveway, Juan and I arrived at a series of yurts connected with wooden decking. In front of the largest was a twelve-foot double cross and behind that a carved birdlike figure that Jonathan calls *águia branca*, or "white eagle." Chairs were set up on the deck in front of the largest yurt. I choose one in the sun and sat down, trying very hard to not think about the fact that I was about to ingest a psychedelic for the first time.

A young father from Portland in his early thirties, whom I'll refer to as Ethan, sat down next to me. He told me he had been to this ceremony several times and had even gone through some mediumship training with Jonathan and his daughter Zara. Ethan asked me what my intention for the weekend was, and I confessed that I didn't really know. When I mentioned I had no experience with other mind-altering substances, he said, "Whoa, really?" and assured me I was in for a wild ride.

When Jonathan arrived, the mood shifted. Speaking and moving slowly, he walked around the group, greeting most with a warm hug. When I told him who I was, he burst into a big smile and grabbed my hands. "You're very welcome. I am glad you're here." That made one of us.

I sat on the deck waiting for someone to tell me what to do. Eventually, Mona, the church member who had done my intake interview the week before, made her way to me. Since she was serving as "guardian" that day, her job was to make sure everyone in the tent was safe and had what they needed. She'd also be taking the Daime, which she told me later made her job easier because she was "in the same energetic field as everyone else."

"Hi Liz! You ready?" Mona said, and before I could protest, she showed me to my spot in the main yurt. To my right was the chair for Mona, another guardian, and "Kathy," a sixty-eight-year-old woman who immediately introduced herself and said, "Daime saved my life." To my left was "Mary," a much less chatty woman with a short white bob, also in her sixties. I set up my space with a BackJack (a low floor chair), a bunch of pillows, and a big white fuzzy blanket.

In the center of the yurt was a low hexagonal table that served as our altar. It held a vase of flowers, a bowl of water, a candle, a double cross, a six-pointed star, and various crystals. Yoga mats and BackJacks were arranged in two sets of semicircles around the altar: a men's side and a women's side. The inner circle was four women and four men, and then behind that was another row where I was one of about ten women against the wall of the yurt. Four guardians flanked the entrance. And on the farthest wall from the entrance was "the family"—Jonathan, Jane, and their adult children Zara and Aaron—as well as musicians and members of the church who would be singing the entire time.

We settled in as Jonathan gave us a bit of introduction about Daime and how the three days would progress.

Drinking Daime, Jonathan told us, is an act of faith, because we're not sure what will happen, but we assume it will be good. And Daime, he reminded us, is not merely a psychedelic. It is also considered a sacrament by the Santo Daime Church.

Our Daime had been made in Brazil through a process that Jonathan explained with the metaphor of ensoulment. The Daime tea is cooked until the divine Spirit enters it. At that point, the tea is simultaneously infused with the body of the divine Spirit and a gateway to other spiritual dimensions. As William Barnard, who is both a religious studies scholar and a Santo Daime initiate, describes it, "By drinking the Daime our physical bodies and the materiality of the Daime conjoin, they commune, until we are, physically and energetically permeated by and suffused with the Christ Consciousness."

Jonathan explained Daime would be offered each day three times. Everyone agreed to drink the first serving. Even me. Then it was up to us if we would drink again, but Jonathan said you should never turn down Daime when offered.

Jonathan described the yurt as a place for healing. We could of course leave but should try to be in the tent as much as possible since it was the safest place to be. Logistics were covered, like where the bathrooms were located and how to use the blue plastic barf bags in a basket at the entrance if needed.

Then it was time to begin. We stood and recited a series of prayers, some in English and some in Portuguese. I recognized the Lord's Prayer and some of the Rosary. Then we exited the main yurt and formed two lines in front of a smaller yurt, one for women and one for men, to receive the Daime. Jonathan served the women, pouring a dark brown liquid from a small glass pitcher into a shot glass with three lines, and then into a small brown paper cup for us to drink in front of him.

By the time I got to Jonathan, my face was wet with stress tears. He smiled and said, "So friend, do you want to dive in?"

"Nope," I responded. "Toe into water, please. I'd like to hold on to the raft for a bit."

And he measured me a serving to the first line. The taste was herbal and medicinal but tolerable.

We were told it could be helpful to set an intention, so I did. "In with joy and adventure, out with fear and control," I breathed. I even went up to the altar and knelt to repeat it. I was going to try everything I could to make my experience a positive one.

About twenty minutes later, it got very quiet in the tent, and then one of the musicians, a young Brazilian man who was reclining on the ground with his guitar, started playing a couple of notes. And we were off to the races.

I had been told not to stare at others, so I tried to look straight ahead, my eyes on the altar. The flower arrangement started to pulsate. The doily covering the altar spun under the items. I closed my eyes to a technicolor kaleidoscope of images and quickly opened them again, feeling more grounded and less dizzy that way.

Several people around me began to twitch and rock, make rapid wrist movements, point fingers, and nod their heads. An elegantly dressed woman in the first row from the back looked like she was bowing, but her movements seemed sped up. A woman to my left was sweeping something away, shaking her head at it. Another woman was on her side under her weighted blanket shaking violently. Several folks gave the impression of physically bracing against the rising sensations.

I heard grunting, squeaking, trilling, laughing, whooping, clapping, clicking, and birdlike whistling. And then the intensity of the music built, and the singing of hymns began. It was a Brazilian syncretic version of what I thought a Pentecostal revival might sound like, at least in terms of the energy and frenzy the hymns created as they became faster and faster in tempo. I was reminded of my experience with sound baths, and instead of blocking out the hymns, I tried to listen as deeply as possible and allow myself to get emotionally carried along.

About another thirty minutes in, I saw Jonathan talking to Jane. His voice traveled surprisingly well in the yurt, and I heard him saying something about how the energy was rising, and he wasn't sure what was coming, but it was their job to help.

And that was when things got wild.

Mary, who was immediately to my left, started to retch into a blue plastic bag. A guardian brought her a clean bag. She retched again, and again. It seemed to go on for almost an hour, sounding increasingly violent. In my altered state, it didn't sound like just throwing up but like something trying to come out, needing to come out.

The next thing that I noticed was "Sarah," a middle-aged woman to my left with long curly hair, popping up in her spot. At first, she swayed a bit, but then she seemed to levitate on her toes. Next, she spun herself into the center of the tent. She knelt and prayed at the altar. She stood as her eyes rolled back into her head. She flicked some unknown contagion off her body and wiped her neck, lower back, arms. She was mumbling something in Portuguese. About ten minutes later, she walked back to her mat and collapsed.

I had witnessed my first medium.

And it wouldn't be my last. Some, like the woman sweeping away something with her hands, were working quietly from their seats. Others had main character energy, like Kathy, the sixty-eight-year old on my right. She jumped up often, stamping her way to the center, squealing, head thrown back, bowing to the altar, then shuffling back to her seat. About thirty minutes later, she was back up again. And again and again.

After the second serving of Daime, my buddy Ethan from Portland got up and really put on a show. He made his way to the center and knelt in front of the altar. Then he poured some of the water on himself and slurped it from his fingers. When he added in some karate kicks and pointed his fingers like guns around the room, I saw Jane and Jonathan look at each other with an amused shake of their heads.

Mediumship is a core practice of the Santo Daime Church. "To be a medium," Jonathan writes in his book *Gift of the Body*, "is to be a bridge between spirit and matter." We all have the potential to be mediums, Jonathan explains, "because we all have a spiritual nature and we all live in a material body." Much as with deep listening, our latent mediumship capacities are suppressed because it is easier to be less sensitive to the energies around us. But the Daime makes that much harder.

Mediumship can take many forms. Some people have visions, others hear voices, others feel energies or emotions that don't originate within themselves. Some forms of mediumship serve the spirits by providing them a way to express themselves and heal. Other forms provide insights or healing to the medium herself. All types of spiritual beings can show up at a Santo Daime ceremony. Sometimes it is a major religious leader, like Jesus or the Virgin Mary. Sometimes it's a deceased individual. Some spirits are healers, some protectors; some are suffering.

At first, the religion scholar in me was delighted by all the displays of mediumship. But when Mona got up, I began to feel differently. Something about Mona forced me to shift from being an observer to being a participant. I'm still not sure why.

I first noticed Mona was bouncing in her guardian seat. Then she made some squeaking noises, jiggling as if being shaken from the inside. When she stood, she began to spin around the altar, her arms swinging over her head in overlapping circles, her long full skirt swirling around her. Then she stopped, stumbled to Jonathan, and knelt before him. Her back, shoulders, and head began shaking. I couldn't see her face, but it was clear she was sobbing.

Mona had seemed so gregarious to me, so upbeat. Very stable and calming. She was part of what was making me feel safe in that tent. But it was clear she still had something she was working through. It was clear she was in pain. And then suddenly I became fixated on that fact that this yurt was full of people who were in pain—enormous pain, some of them. In my altered state, I was convinced I was having a deep insight, but it wasn't a pleasant one. My big epiphany was that PTSD was so common it was the defining factor of being human. I couldn't stop focusing on that idea and started to spontaneously weep myself.

In the middle of all that, Jonathan caught my eye. As soon as Mona sat down, he walked over to me, knelt on my mat, and smiled. I looked at him, still blubbering, and smiled back.

"Are you ready for more Daime, friend?" he asked.

I shook my head no.

"Are you sure?"

I nodded a vigorous yes.

But he wasn't having it. "Let me tell you what I see. I see you struggling. The Daime will make it easier."

I really did look like I was unraveling, and I thought, *Fine.*

This is why I'm here. I gave an unenthusiastic "OK," which was all he needed. He headed out of the tent, and I reluctantly followed. I was grateful that he gave me a small dose. And he was right. Within a few minutes, my crying stopped.

The climax of act 1 came toward the end of the day, after everyone (except me) had consumed a third serving of Daime. Sarah, who had popped up early in the day, was back in the center by the altar and had been for what seemed like a long time. She was bowing to the cross, sprinkling something unseen on the flowers, raising her hands up above her head, and dancing slowly in circles. Since we were about to close out the work for the day, Zara got up from her seat and approached Sarah. At first, Zara just stood next to her and held her hand. But when Zara tried to lead her back to her seat, Sarah made a loud noise, stiffened, and pulled back. Zara whispered something, and Sarah responded with a snarl and dramatically fell to the ground. Zara backed away, and Jonathan and Jane rushed over. Both were speaking in low, calm voices to her. Something about "It's time to go." Sarah let out more protests and stiffened on the ground as Jonathan's voice got firmer. He made a *szut szut* sound while making a hand motion from her chest upward, as if pulling something out of her, and finally she relaxed. The entire episode was over in a couple of minutes, and everyone settled back into our seats.

To end the ceremony, we stood and recited the series of prayers again. We went out onto the deck to snack on blueberry muffins Jane had baked for us, the first time we had been allowed to eat all day, and then we returned to the tent for a period of sharing. Jonathan mentioned the episode with Sarah, referring to it as an exorcism. It was a bit shocking to hear him use that word so casually. He shared that he was part of a group helping the Oregon Health Authority set protocols for psilocybin treatment centers and facilitators in the state since it is now legal in licensed settings. He joked that if the episode with Sarah occurred in a clinical setting, the guidelines his group had developed would require a facilitator to immediately call the police. But in the religious context of that yurt, a bit of hand-holding, some firm words, a series of energy work zapping, and it was all over.

After a shared communal meal, Juan and I headed back to our hotel. "Liz, you were lucky," he said. "There was really a lot going on in the tent today." No kidding. And let me just say that when you are on ayahuasca and the person next to you thinks they're purging something evil, channeling a spirit, or performing an exorcism, it seems very plausible that they are. And I still had two more days to go.

Act 2: A Plot Twist

I had decided that the second day, I would take more Daime. But when I got up to Jonathan for my first serving, I chickened out and asked for the smallest serving again. He said, "I think you should have more . . . to go deeper."

I agreed to a second-line serving, emptying my cup in front of him.

"Good for you," he said. As I walked away, he added, "Bless you."

Today Jonathan told us they were going to try something a bit unusual and sing the St. Michael Hymns. At the time I had no idea what that meant but later read that these hymns are focused on helping suffering and obsessing spirits. Perhaps that is why the mood felt darker.

This time, my initial wave of visions was more intense and lasted longer. Some of the men's faces looked sinister to me, and whenever one of them yawned, they seemed to morph into a demon. I breathed as slowly and deeply as I could so I wouldn't panic. I chugged from my water bottle, hoping that would move the Daime through my system quicker. I was still struggling to feel in control when the offer for the second serving came.

That was how I came to be lying in the tent on my mat, eyes closed, while folks were outside on the deck letting the second serving of Daime start to settle. And I overheard a conversation between Jonathan and Mona. "She's very upset and threatening to go home," Mona said. "She feels like men have always told her she was doing things wrong."

Jonathan responded, "I told her what I saw. She asked me if any of it was real and I said some, but very little. You don't need to jump up every ten minutes. That is about her need to be important. It's not doing the work."

I realized that Kathy had been missing from the yurt for most of the morning.

Jonathan continued in a lower voice, but I caught "He's trying so hard it's cartoonish." Suddenly the amused head shake Jane and Jonathan had shared during Ethan's karate kicks made more sense.

That was when I realized Jonathan and his family had been trying to guide the mediums all day. Jonathan describes mediumship as being composed of inspiration, ego, and drama. The challenge is to properly discern which one is bubbling up at a particular time and to resist instances motivated by self-importance or performance. Helping mediums with that correct discernment was part of his family's job in the tent. That included Jonathan's verbal scolding, to be sure, but I had also noticed Zara stand up and prevent Sarah from moving toward the altar a couple of times and block Ethan when he started pointing gun fingers around the room again. They had been teaching the mediums and protecting the integrity of the ceremony.

About an hour into everyone else's second serving, I was silently crying again. Jonathan made his way over to me. "So it's that time again, friend. I've come to offer you another serving of Daime."

"No, thank you," I said. "I'm good."

"Well, I can only tell you what I see," he said. "I see something bubbling up. Something you could release. You don't need the Daime to let it go, but the Daime will help."

"I'd rather just release it without the Daime," I said.

He nodded and went back to his seat.

Because I had just promised to try to release something, I let myself think about the one thing I had told myself I would not think about while on ayahuasca. I thought of my dad.

What I allowed myself to think about was not that he had died a little over a year before. To lose a parent is a normal part of life, and I had always felt like I was on borrowed time with my dad, who had been a heavy smoker, a lifelong drinker, and medicated for high cholesterol and blood pressure. He'd had a heart attack and quadruple bypass in his midsixties and was diagnosed with Parkinson's in his seventies. And that was all before the pancreatic cancer that eventually killed him.

I didn't dwell on his pain during the last year of his life when he suffered from the side effects of chemo and never really recovered from a Whipple surgery. I think that was also something I had come to terms with.

Instead, I allowed myself to close my eyes, listen to the hymn, and think about what I really don't like to think about: the night he passed.

In the months leading up to my father's death, he'd had a series of blood infections that landed him in the hospital. After the last infection, he'd been too weak for my stepmother to take care of him at home, so they checked him into a rehab hospital. In hindsight, it was clear he was already transitioning by the time he got there. Besides being very weak, he was hallucinating, and would often describe what he was seeing crawling on his ceiling or hiding in the corners to my sister and me. There was a squirrel who would come in and out of the vent at the foot of his bed and spiders in the corners. There was an intense man in a black suit with eyeglasses, and a translucent woman who was glowing. He'd often say to us, "You can't see that, right?" We would reassure him there was nothing there and then bring up some pleasant memory from our childhood. A few days into that rehab stay, he saw his oncologist, who said it was time to go home and begin hospice care.

That night after he got home, my stepmother called to say he had taken a sharp turn for the worse, and within the hour, I was driving to their home in New Hampshire. When I got there, I found her almost hysterical and a hospice nurse who said immediately, "I'm glad you came." For the next five hours, my stepmother and I sat with my father in his bed and I administered the morphine per the nurse's instructions. It wasn't a peaceful passing. He was in pain until his last breath. Agitated. Scared. I'd even say panicked. I'm glad I was with him, but it was not a good death. And admitting that is what I released, at least a bit, in the tent.

That experience reminded me of a 2023 *New York Times Magazine* interview with the late Roland Griffiths, a professor of psychopharmacology who led the Center for Psychedelic and Consciousness Research at Johns Hopkins University for decades. In that interview, conducted six months before he died of colon cancer, he shared how studying psychedelics and then taking them—LSD, in his case—helped him personally to come to terms with his diagnosis. Instead of feeling fear or dread, he felt "transcendently positive feelings about existence" and "the great mystery of consciousness." "We all know that we're terminal," Griffiths told *The New York Times*. "In principle we shouldn't need this Stage 4 cancer diagnosis to awaken." Psychedelics, administered in the proper set and setting, can, in Griffiths's words, "shake the bars and tell people, 'Come on, let's wake up!'"

This sort of aha moment is a common way to describe the consciousness raising of psychedelic experiences. But there was something else in that interview that I couldn't put a finger on until my Daime experience. It was how Griffiths was describing psychedelics as a form of training for how to confront the most mysterious aspects of life, including death. As Griffiths put it, psychedelics facilitate not only feel-good experiences but also frightening ones. The key, Griffiths thought, is to learn how "to stay with them, be curious and recognize the ephemeral nature of them." Being able to do that seemed like helpful preparation for my own eventual death and the deaths of my loved ones. I certainly think it could have allowed my dad and me to reframe his hallucinations as visions and be more curious about them than scared of them.

Act 3: Integration

I woke up on the third day feeling dizzy with a strong sense of vertigo. I decided I was going to protect myself and drink very little Daime, even if that meant I was going to "do it wrong." When Jonathan offered me the first serving of the day, I dipped my tongue in, grimaced, and walked away. Ten minutes later, I disposed of my paper cup when no one was looking.

And yet, that day turned out to be the most intense for me. It began with a lot of crying. The Daime had me; I was what Daime initiates call *pegado.* I wasn't sad but raw, as if I had been emotionally split open. I found myself physically reacting to the energetic and spiritual work of others, and that freaked me out.

Let me give some examples. About halfway through the

day, everyone else was well into their second dose of Daime. I was lying on my mat, almost asleep, exhausted from all the overstimulation of the last two days. But suddenly something happened in the tent. I didn't see it happen, I felt it, like a jolt that caused me to shudder. I sat up and tried to figure out what was going on. To my left, someone let out a little squeal. I realized Jonathan was zapping his energy work on a young woman sitting two people away from me. It looked like he was pulling and pushing things from and to her. Had something hit me by mistake? But what would that be?

Later, when the male guitarist was in the center by the altar engaging in mediumship, I again felt waves of something hitting me. I began breathing very heavily, and a guardian had to restock the box of tissues in front of me.

But the worst of it was another reaction I had to Mona.

That day, Mona was one of the singers, while someone else took over the guardianship duties. I had seen her sort of jiggle and spasm a bit in her seat, but nothing very dramatic. At some point in the afternoon, I got up and left the tent to use the bathroom. And while I was gone, something happened, which I only know because several people made reference to "Mona's episode" during the group share at the end of the day. I didn't see any of it.

But I did feel it. I was outside the tent when it all went down, trying to return, and I could not physically climb the steps to the deck. Something wouldn't let me. I tried three times and only made it up one step, holding on to the handrail like it was the only thing keeping me upright. *What the heck?* I thought at the time.

Then Mona and Jonathan appeared at the door of the yurt. They were heading for the large double cross, a place Jonathan often did some of his most intense healing work. I looked away and leaned into the railing as they passed by me. Having them behind me suddenly propelled me up the stairs, but I didn't want to enter the tent. Instead, I sat in a deck chair right next to the wall of the yurt, avoiding looking at Mona and Jonathan, who were about twenty feet from me at the cross. I again felt waves of what I can only describe as emotional energy hitting me, but this time they were at a new level of intensity.

I started to breathe very heavily. I was sobbing again. I clenched the armrests of my chair, eyes closed, trying to force myself to calm down. But no luck. It went on for about ten minutes, until, I guess, Mona finished whatever she was doing with Jonathan at the cross. The waves of sensations I was feeling stopped all at once. They returned to the tent, and I followed.

I had Jonathan's voice in the back of my head saying that sometimes newcomers don't realize they have mediumship sensitivities. I spent the rest of the day trying not to think about what that might mean for me.

To wrap up that last day, we spent some time on what in the world of psychedelics is called integration.

Rabbi Art Green, who first experienced LSD with Leary's Harvard group when he was a rabbinical student, thinks part of the challenge of psychedelics is that they can facilitate a mystical experience almost too quickly. "The problem is that if someone has that experience after twenty years of meditation, there's a certain gravitas to that experience." And that gravitas is missing if you "pop a pill." Put differently, psychedelics might push us off the platform of everyday consciousness into something more, but that's the easy part. As Green puts it, "The experience is not difficult, but bringing it back into reality is what it's all about." Integration is the work of "bringing it back."

The religious aspects of the Daime ceremony were helpful for this process. There was a supportive group—many of whom were Daime initiates—to share their insights. During the last share, almost everyone had something to say. There was a man who told us of how the Daime had helped him forgive his dad. Another shared he had begun to heal a family fissure that morning with a ceremony-inspired phone call. A teacher had learned she shouldn't overinvest in her students. Someone shared a lovely poem they had written. Several people expressed gratitude for the healing they had received. Then—and this shocked me—Ethan and Kathy both confessed how they had been scolded by Jonathan for "faking mediumship" and how that had forced them both to take a hard look at themselves.

To help with integration, there was also a discussion of how to adjust our patterns of behavior going forward, including something Jonathan called a new agreement, or *novo acordo.* "How would we bring back to our everyday lives what we learned in the tent?" he asked. We are, as Jonathan explained using a Buddhist term, householders, with families and jobs. We are in the world. That world calls us to an agreement, but after the Daime ceremony, we should revise that agreement. "What is it like to live in that world and bring what is transforming in you to it? You can't know what it will look like, but you can be more intentional about your heart. And don't be cavalier about setting your new agreement. The Beings take you very seriously. You should as well." And finally, he left us with the following question before the closing prayers: "What is your homework?"

The invitation to write a *novo acordo* made it clear this weekend was not supposed to be a shortcut. A jumpstart perhaps, but not a shortcut. The entire point was to learn how to live differently, more fully, how to show up for our friends, family, and communities in better ways. To experience all the benefits to our well-being, we would have to go home and continue to put in the work. This is the real purpose of our time together, in the words of psychologist Robert Ornstein: altered traits, not just altered states.

And then it was all over, except our last communal dinner. I sat across from Jonathan, too tired to make small talk. When Juan said it was time to go, I looked at Jonathan, and he asked, "So?"

"Easiest fieldwork I've ever done," I joked, and then blurted out, "Today was really hard for me. I was physically reacting to things in the tent. And that was overwhelming."

"Did you know that about yourself?" he asked.

"Know what?"

"That you're sensitive to others' energy?"

"Huh. Well, I guess I would have said I'm emotionally sensitive, but no, I wouldn't have described myself as sensitive to energy," I said. *In part, because I don't believe in that,* I added silently.

Jonathan got serious. "I think you learned something really profound about yourself this weekend, and something you can apply to how you react to others."

I made a throwaway comment about picking up on my teenage daughter's mood, but Jonathan said, "Yes, exactly. Look, there were hundreds of things going on in that tent today, and you reacted to only a handful. Like attracts like, so something about that energy was resonating with something inside you."

I thanked him again for allowing me to attend. His final words to me were, "You're going to figure out more in the coming days what happened here."

RESTORING RELIGION TO PSYCHEDELICS

Are psychedelics for me? I don't think so. I'm not itching for another mind-altering experience anytime soon. But am I glad my first experience was in a religious community? Absolutely. And was it meaningful, ethical, and effective? One hundred percent. Was that the religion? I think so.

If I take a step back and think collectively about the religious aspects of my experience, I can see at least three ways they helped me. One, they made ingesting a psychedelic feel less risky, which allowed me to lean into the experience more. Two, they provided a way to make sense of what happened in that tent. And three, they helped me begin to integrate my insights into my normal life.

I am still unconvinced that psychedelics are harmless. People have psychotic breaks while using them. Some even die. I know psychedelics are surging in popularity, but I think this might be because their risks are being downplayed. So I was really concerned that ayahuasca would be anti-therapeutic for me, which is to say, I might have a bad trip. The religion of the Daime ceremony felt like a way to mitigate that risk.

I have deep respect for Jonathan and his family, and because of that I invested them with quite a bit of trust. I still can't believe that after one Zoom conversation with Jonathan, I was booking a flight to take ayahuasca in a yurt in Oregon. But Jonathan promised me I would be safe. I believed him. And he was right.

The ceremony was hosted by members of the Church of the Holy Light of the Queen. I was comforted by that fact that this wasn't a recreational fad to them, but rather part of a century-old tradition of work. I liked that I was in a group of people who consumed Daime regularly and who had a lot of experience with what could happen. And I saw how that expertise came in handy when Jonathan had to perform an exorcism on Sarah. As Jonathan told us, that same incident in a clinical setting would have been framed as a psychotic break, and the police would have been called. In that tent, the episode was caused by a spirit being, not a mental breakdown, and it was dealt with relatively easily.

In a clinical setting, the incident would have been framed as a psychotic break. In the tent, it was caused by a spirit being, and it was dealt with relatively easily.

The guardians, whom I like to think of as the deacons of the Daime, really contributed to my feeling of safety. They took care of us all. They held back hair while people purged outside. They supplied pillows and tissues to those who needed them. They made sure everyone leaving the tent had either a known destination or a companion. Everyone felt seen in that yurt; their process, whatever it was, was witnessed. That felt comforting on many levels.

The work Jonathan and Zara did to reel in some of the more performative forms of mediumship also made me trust that tricksters would not be tolerated in that ceremonial space. Their guidance did not feel controlling in the way religious leadership is sometimes characterized. Rather, it provided some guardrails. And I'm not convinced the integrity of psychedelic experiences that occur outside religious traditions, communities, and institutions is protected in the same way.

Finally, there were ritual aspects of the ceremony that I found grounding. The altar was one of them. I believed Jonathan when he told us that the altar was for us to use in whatever way we chose. Setting my intention while kneeling at the altar before we began made the intention stick a bit more. It gave me a place to focus when things got a bit frenzied in the tent. The hymns also felt like a lifeline. They raised and lowered the energy in the tent but also provided something for me to hold on to. Even though I was unable to sing along and did not even understand most of the words, they guided the work. They were a way to ride the wave instead of getting stuck in the churn.

A feeling of safety allowed me to learn from what the Daime brought up for me, at least more than I would have otherwise. I certainly credit the religious context with encouraging me to think about my father's death, something I hadn't realized I had experienced as traumatic until that weekend.

There were also concepts and frameworks that helped me make sense of what happened in the yurt. The doctrine of mediumship had the most influence on me. Witnessing it made it feel like the Daime was manifesting the divine in some real way.

The revelation that there were some less than sincere mediums in our midst didn't undermine the power of this idea for me. On the contrary, seeing fake mediums being called out—and then, even more incredibly, seeing them confess to "performing" based on erroneous discernment and ego—made me more convinced that other forms of mediumship that weekend were indeed real in a meaningful way. And, frankly, few experiences can convince you of the reality of spiritual beings like tripping in a yurt full of practicing mediums.

Mediumship also affected how I interpreted my own emotional and physical reactions that weekend. I first worried, but then accepted, that the Daime made me extra sensitive to the emotions and unseen forms of energy of others, especially Mona's. I started to buy into the idea that we are all potentially mediums.

I didn't think of it until about a week after the ceremony, but my grandfather heard voices, I think most of his life. This was surprising for me to learn, given he was a mechanical engineer who developed turbines for General Electric, always wore a belt and button-down shirt, and was a proud New Englander with hobbies like canoe building. He was the least religious or woo-woo person I have ever known. And yet, when my cousin being treated for schizophrenia said he was hearing voices, some of which were telling him to do bad things, I remember my grandfather saying, "That's ridiculous. Everyone hears voices. Just don't listen to them."

I don't hear voices like my grandfather, but I do pick up on what happens around me. And I left that weekend curious about how I might apply this insight to my everyday life. Could I learn to respond to others with compassion instead of empathy, since the later leads to me internalizing the sadness and stress of others as my own? Surely that would help my well-being.

When I think about how I carried that experience forward, two things come to mind. The first was that, as part of my *novo acordo*, I resolved to try to be less reactive to those around me as a way to acknowledge my newly discovered energetic sensitivities. I did manage to calmly navigate a blowup between my partner and teenage daughter the day I got home from Oregon by keeping this in mind and focusing on patience. But honestly, I've been less successful in the months that have followed.

The second thing I brought back into everyday life was a new interest in the purpose of dying and what a good death might look like. *What would it mean to approach death with acceptance, openness, and courage? To see the process of death as a necessary part of life, not its enemy? To prepare with friends and family in ways that are comforting and affirming to them?* It might have been a psychedelic that raised these questions, but religion is where I am looking for possible answers.

I am considering resurrecting (pun intended) the Meaning of Death course for my department, which used to be our most highly enrolled religion course, but hasn't been regularly taught for years. And I have looked into becoming a death doula as a way to serve others. But mostly I'm open to the idea that religions have lots of resources to help me navigate this final human adventure and recognize I have only begun to scratch the surface.

While I do think religion deepened my psychedelic experience, I am convinced it could have done even more, had I allowed it. Take the central doctrine of Santo Daime, that Daime is a sacrament. I understand intellectually and theologically what is at stake with this designation, but I never fully embraced the idea. To me the Daime remained, to some extent, a drug. (Thanks, Nancy Reagan.) Occasionally I saw it as a form of medicine for healing, but never fully as a vehicle for accessing the divine. That meant I couldn't experience all it had to teach me. Day three was a case in point. I was dizzy and overwhelmed, and I avoided consuming more than a sip of the Daime because of it. If I had accepted the Daime as a sacrament, that would have been the very time to dive in deeper and ingest more Daime, trusting that whatever happened next was what needed to happen. And I'm a bit disappointed with myself that I didn't do that.

When I got home, my partner, Alexis, asked if I'd ever consider taking psychedelics again for reasons other than research. I said not recreationally, but I could imagine participating in another Daime ceremony for one of two reasons.

The first was if I needed to process a terrible loss, like if he died. I imagine the Daime could help. As Jonathan had told me, I didn't need the Daime to release whatever I was holding on to, but it would make that release easier.

The second reason I told him I might return was if I got a terminal diagnosis. Not because I thought Daime would cure me, but because I believed it could help teach me how to die well. And what could be more important to well-being than that?

Conclusion

Restoring the Religious Roots of Spiritual Practices

I'm lying on my mat in savasana, staring at the ceiling of a high-end studio in Tribeca, having paid seventy dollars to guarantee a spot in a class with this particular wellness guru. And I'm noticing a black discoloration around all the vents and light fixtures. Did I just spend sixty minutes engaged in somatic movement to release stuck energy in a room with black mold? If so, it would be a good metaphor for the type of spirituality the wellness industry offers.

When we visit their spiritual salad bar, it's like we are piling our plates with kale and organic tofu because someone told us these items are good for us. But then we discover the kale is contaminated with salmonella. Or we're allergic to soy. Or we drown the entire salad in ultra-processed blue cheese dressing to make it taste better, canceling out the nutritional benefits. Similarly, when we try on spiritual practices, removed from their full context, and combine them into a hodgepodge self-care routine, sometimes we're working against ourselves.

But the wellness industry isn't entirely to blame. Part of this situation we created because of our deep distrust of religious institutions, leaders, and dogma. We want the watered-down version of religion that wellness influencers hawk because we think it will be safer for us and more consistent with our values. But that's not always the case. Spiritual wellness practices can cause real harm—I'm thinking of meditation sickness, a bad trip at an ayahuasca retreat, or a detox diet that valorizes thinness at all costs. They can conflict with our core values—for example, when we unknowingly prostrate ourselves to a god whom we don't believe in during a Sun Salutation or participate in a spiritual exercise class that is only available to the few who can afford the hefty price tag.

There is a bigger problem. By ignoring the religious context and content of these practices, we're leaving a lot on the table. Those religious worldviews, systems of values, and visions of what it means to be human have something to teach us as well. Religions are the OG wellness influencers, after all.

We have seen several ways in which restoring religion to popular spiritual wellness practices can give them more purpose, responsibility, and efficacy. For instance:

- Yoga's religious roots can reframe a daily flow into an opportunity to cultivate embodied virtues.

- Monastic meditation encourages us to think about mindfulness as social engagement, not just personal therapy.

- AA's idea of a higher power is an invitation to consider how accepting that we are not-God might improve our lives.

- Holistic religious foodways offer alternatives to the diet industry's obsession with fasting, toxins, and thinness.

- Mantra-based group exercise that is inclusive and offers a version of leadership beyond a celebrity guru can create a real sense of belonging.

- Sacred sound experiences can remake us into sensitive listeners who are better at discerning the world around us.

- Religious ceremonies can transform a psychedelic trip into a way to confront the existential crisis of death.

To access those insights, we have to approach religion in a new way—especially those of us who don't identify as religious at all. We don't have to join a church, withdraw into a monastery, or adopt dogma that conflicts with our core values and sense of self, but we do have to stop treating religion as a repository of techniques of self-care. Instead, religion must become a conversation partner. A conversation partner who has grappled with what a full human life might entail for centuries and who is trying to help us figure out what it might entail for us today. A conversation partner who challenges our assumptions about what is, what could be, and often what should be true.

This is how we get beyond wellness to something much deeper. Sometimes referred to as "flourishing," "following the right path," or even "salvation," it's what I call real well-being.

It is a meaning-making, value-driven process of discerning and acting in relationship with others and the world. It is about living better by living lives that are as fully human as possible.

This book told the stories I collected as I tried to take more seriously the religious roots of the spiritual practices I am drawn to. I have learned a lot from this experiment, sometimes from religious communities and individuals, sometimes from scholarly studies, and sometimes from firsthand experiences embedded in a tradition. There is certainly more to discover, but here are my top ten religious insights into real well-being:

1. **Community is central.** Religions think of well-being as a collective pursuit and teach us that it is grounded in social values, relationships, and responsibilities, not just personal achievement or gratification.

2. **Ethics are not optional.** While wellness might focus on alleviating individual suffering, real well-being comes with ethical obligations to others, to the divine, or to the natural world around us. A good life is a moral life.

3. **Powerful practices come with risk.** If a practice is powerful enough to help, it is powerful enough to hurt. Religious ideas, interpretations, and rituals provide guardrails for powerful practices based on a community's centuries of experience.

4. **Get informed to be transformed.** Learning from faith leaders, religious community members, or religious studies scholars is a great way to get to know the "ingredient list" of spiritual practices so that they can work better for us.

5. **There is a role for discipline.** Our efficiency-obsessed culture encourages us to find shortcuts to everything, including our own well-being. Religions, in contrast, often teach there is value in the slow, hard, and messy aspects of life. Or, as Bhante G might say, we should dig fewer, but deeper, holes.

6. **Value alignment matters.** Practices create and reinforce values, remaking us into (hopefully) better versions of ourselves. It is important to be sure the values associated with the practices we adopt align with our own core values, otherwise we risk moral injury.

7. **Develop life skills.** A religiously informed version of well-being is not simply a fixed self-care routine. Instead it requires an ongoing process of learning skills like cultivating virtues, improving discernment, and building more resilient communities.

8. **Give up the illusion of control.** Religious worldviews push back on the intoxicating idea that we can master our own well-being. They remind us we are not-God, which means we can't completely fix ourselves with life hacks.

9. **The goal is not perfection.** If much of the wellness industry promises us perfection—whether that's thinness, beauty, happiness, enhanced cognitive function, or longevity—religions encourage us to acknowledge the vulnerability of human life and accept our imperfections as part of being fully human. For religions, well-being isn't about finding a cure for

the human condition; it is a way to heal and flourish within our limitations.

10. **Change the world.** Spirituality that ignores questions of social justice is a sedative. For real well-being, we must imagine and create a better world for ourselves and others.

For me, being middle-aged has meant a lot of life changes in the last couple of years, including losing my father, preparing for my daughter to leave for college, and dealing with all the effects of perimenopause, like night sweats and joint pain. And that's not even mentioning the enormous political and economic uncertainty in the United States. I am writing this during the beginning of Trump's second term in office. My partner is a federal employee at risk of losing his job. Aggressive tariffs and budget cuts have wreaked havoc on the stock market and disrupted my retirement plans. And higher education, the sector that employs me, is under attack.

You might also feel like you're living through uncertain times and grappling with how best to respond.

We all could use some roots right now. And religion offers some deep ones.

I don't want to ignore the fact that the religious institutions we inherited have failed many of us, or that religious values are being used to justify major political changes in the United States, many of which I don't agree with. *But could we harness religion in a different way to help imagine a better future?*

My journey might not be yours, but for me the religious insights into real well-being have been less about some supernatural reality or debates about the existence of God, and much more about a thicker understanding of human nature. We have the capacity to be deep listeners but have forgotten it. We are not-God despite acting like we are. We are drawn to the mystery and consciousness that is beyond our everyday experience but need help to integrate that into our normal lives. We crave community but have forgotten that a real community asks something from us in return. These insights strike me as important beacons as we try to figure out what we believe and who we want to be, and work hard not to let the loudest voices control the story of who we are and who we will become.

Acknowledgments

Writing *Beyond Wellness* has been a deeply personal, occasionally disorienting, and surprisingly joyful ride. I owe thanks to a whole crew of generous souls who helped bring this book into being.

First, to my agent, Mark Tauber, who convinced me it was finally time to write my first trade book. Your guidance, shrewd business instincts, and friendship made the process of proposing and writing this book fun. And certainly, this book would not exist without you.

To the team at Tarcher: Thank you for believing in this project and helping shape it with such care and insight. Your support made this book better at every stage. This is especially true of Lauren O'Neal, my editor extraordinaire: Your enthusiasm for this project was not only contagious—it was necessary. You helped me believe this book could live in the world as something both smart and readable, and I'm forever grateful for your vision and guidance.

To my marketing coach, Jenn Jensen of Copilot Publishing: Thank you for helping me see that doing what I love in public is the best—and most enjoyable—form of self-promotion.

To the spiritual wellness practitioners who generously agreed to be interviewed: Thank you for trusting me with your stories and insights. A heartfelt thanks especially to Rania Awaad, Bhante G, Bhante S, Michelle Garside, Jonathan Goldman, Liz Kineke, Don Lattin, Ashley Mitchell, Lucy Osborne, Natalia Mehlman Petrzela, "Vicki," and "Melanie"—your wisdom made this book richer and truer.

To my colleagues in religious studies: Thank you for doing the hard work of thinking seriously about religion in all its weird and wonderful forms. I have tried to cite as many of you as possible to share your work with new readers. Natalie Avalos, Nalika Gajaweera, Ira Helderman, Mike Hogue, Grace Kao, Irene Oh, and Simran Jeet Singh had important conversations with me about this material, read early drafts, and offered the kind of honest, incisive feedback that only true friends and scholars can provide. A special shout-out to Ann Gleig and Kirsten Wesselhoeft—you two went far above and beyond what anyone expects of colleagues and often on a very short timeline. The generosity and intellectual companionship of my colleagues have meant the world to me.

I'm grateful to the John Templeton Foundation for their grant to support the Spirituality and the Ethics of Religious Borrowing project, which allowed me to create a collaborative research group that infused new energy into this book in its final stages. To Northeastern University—thank you for giving me the space, resources, and community to pursue this work with seriousness and imagination. And to the Northeastern students who brainstormed, researched, and annotated—Maya Rabow, Olivia Sedarksi, and Elizabeth Thorne—you were my research dream team. I hope this book carries traces of your curiosity and care.

To my family: Thank you for putting up with my many research trips, strange reading material, and extended monologues about obscure spiritual trends. A special thank-you to my sisters and sister-in-law, who listened patiently as I processed some of the more personal stories in these pages—you helped me make sense of it all. And to my partner, Alexis: Thank you for understanding that I needed to wake up at five a.m. every day to write, for covering meals when I was deep in a deadline spiral, and for gently reminding me that sunlight and fresh air are, in fact, good for writers. You are better than anyone I know at living life to its fullest—and in your own way, you've always embodied what *Beyond Wellness* is really about. You're constantly (and patiently) trying to get me to do the same.

Notes

CHAPTER 1: BENDY BODIES

10 **It was dubbed:** Eileen Luhr, "Seeker, Surfer, Yogi: The Progressive Religious Imagination and the Cultural Politics of Place in Encinitas, California," *American Quarterly* (2015): 1173–78.

10 **It was a way:** Luhr, "Seeker, Surfer, Yogi," 1185.

12 **according to Sedlock's book:** Jennifer Sedlock, *The Yoga Crisis in America* (Maitland, FL: Xulon Press Elite, 2019), 4.

12 **And to many parents:** Candy Gunther Brown, *Debating Yoga and Mindfulness in Public Schools* (Chapel Hill, NC: University of North Carolina Press, 2019), 121.

12 **They collected 250 signatures:** Sedlock, *The Yoga Crisis in America*, 22.

12 **Broyles, a local attorney:** Dean Broyles, "About Us," The National Center for Law Policy, https://nclplaw.org/about-us/.

13 **Broyles filed a complaint:** Dean Broyles, "Verified Petition for Writ of Mandamus; Complaint for Injunctive and Declaratory Relief," *Sedlock*, February 20, 2013.

13 **Meyer actually found:** John Meyer, "Statement of Decision," *Sedlock*, July 1, 2013 (oral), September 23, 2013 (final).

13 **Although Meyer agreed:** Meyer, "Statement of Decision."

14 **"We assume, without deciding":** Meyer, "Statement of Decision."

15 **Meyer went as far:** Meyer, "Statement of Decision."

15 **"Ashtanga is grounded":** Candy Gunther Brown, *Debating Yoga and Mindfulness in Public Schools*, 116. Emphasis in the original.

16 **The difference, Brown points out:** Brown, *Debating Yoga and Mindfulness in Public Schools*, 117.

16 **But as religious studies scholar:** Amanda Lucia, *White Utopias* (Oakland: University of California Press, 2020), 93.

16 **So many Americans read:** Lucia, *White Utopias,* 93.

19 **"It will help businessmen":** Indra Devi, *Yoga for Americans* (Whitefish, MT: Kessinger Publishing, 2010), xii.

20 **The movement appealed:** Hugh Urban, *New Age, Neopagan, and New Religious Movements* (Berkeley: University of California Press, 2015), 213.

22 **In 1998, Goswami Kriyananda:** YJ Editors, "The Yoga Teacher Who Brought Yoga to Our Living Rooms Decades Before Online Yoga Was a Thing," *Yoga Journal,* March 3, 2023, https://www.yogajournal.com/yoga-101/philosophy/lilias-folan-yoga-s-grande-dame/.

22 **As *Time* magazine put it:** Stefanie Syman, *The Subtle Body: The Story of Yoga in America* (New York: Farrar, Straus and Giroux, 2010), 248.

23 **It adds acoustic gravitas:** Kumari Devarajan, "How 'Namaste' Flew Away from Us," *Code Switch: Word Watch,* January 17, 2020, https://www.npr.org/sections/codeswitch/2020/01/17/406246770/how-namaste-flew-away-from-us.

24 **The most popular reason:** "Yoga in the World Research Study," Yoga Affairs, accessed July 16, 2025, https://r.yogaalliance.org/Yoga_in_the_World.

27 **In fact, Jois once told:** K. Pattabhi Jois interview by Alexander Medin, "3 Gurus, 48 Questions: Matching Interviews with Sri T. K. V. Desikachar, Sri B. K. S. Iyengar and Sri K. Pattabhi Jois," ed. Deirdre Summerbell, *Namarupa* (Fall 2004): 18.

27 **"The keystone teaching":** Richard Faulds, *Kripalu Yoga: A Guide to Practice On and Off the Mat* (New York: Bantam Books, 2005), 182.

30 **Well-known yoga activist:** Susanna Barkataki (@susannabarkataki), Instagram post, May 23, 2022.

30 **And what can we do:** Susanna Barkataki, *Embrace Yoga's Roots: Courageous Ways to Deepen Your Yoga Practice* (Orlando, FL: Ignite Yoga and Wellness Institute, 2020), 10–12, 179.

30 **For Barkataki, the way:** Barkataki, *Embrace Yoga's Roots,* 45–52.

CHAPTER 2: MIND CURE

34 **This was a minor:** Northeastern University, "Mindfulness Minor, Overview," Course Catalog, https://catalog.northeastern.edu/undergraduate/health-sciences/community-health-behavioral-sciences/mindfulness-minor/.

34 **"It worked for some":** MYRIAD Project, "What did we find?," https://myriadproject.org/what-we-did/what-did-we-find/.

35 **Hallucinations and dizziness:** Cheetah House, "Symptoms," https://www.cheetahhouse.org/symptoms.

35 **One study found:** Marco Schlosser et al., "Unpleasant meditation-related experiences in regular meditators: Prevalence, predictors, and conceptual considerations," *PLoS One* 14.5 (2019): e0216643, https://doi.org/10.1371/journal.pone.0216643.

35 **She frames meditation sickness:** Willoughby Britton, "Can mindfulness be too much of a good thing? The value of a middle way," *Current Opinion in Psychology* 28 (2019): 159.

35 **For instance, although mindfulness:** Britton, "Can mindfulness be too much of a good thing?," 160.

35 **And while mindfulness:** Britton, "Can mindfulness be too much of a good thing?," 160.

35 **Similarly, some mindfulness:** Willoughby Britton et al., "Awakening is not a metaphor: The effects of Buddhist meditation practices on basic wakefulness," *Annals of the New York Academy of Sciences* 1307 (2014): 64–81.

36 **And that is why:** Correspondence with the author via email, March 21, 2025. See also Ira Helderman, "'Meditation madness': Meditation's popularity, popular religion and unsupervised religion," *Culture and Religion*, December 21, 2023.

36 **It is a quick:** Miles Neale, Buddhist and psychotherapist, is credited with coining the term "McMindfulness." See his 2010 interview with Danny Fisher, "Frozen Yoga and McMindfulness: Miles Neale on the mainstreaming of contemplative religious practices," *Lion's Roar*, December 15, 2010, https://www.lionsroar.com/frozen-yoga-and-mcmindfulness-miles-neale-on-the-mainstreaming-of-contemplative-religious-practices.

36 **I first encountered:** For instance, Jared Lindahl et al., "The roles and impacts of worldviews in the context of meditation-related challenges," *Transcultural Psychiatry* 60.4 (2023): 637–50, and Roman Palitsky et al., "Relationships Between Religious and Scientific Worldviews in the Narratives of Western Buddhists Reporting Meditation-Related Challenges," *Journal of Contemplative Studies* (April 13, 2023): 1–28.

37 **Geertz famously described:** Clifford Geertz, "Religion as a Cultural System," in *The Interpretation of Cultures: Selected Essays* (New York: Basic Books, 1973), 87–125.

37 **In other words:** Roman Palitsky et al., "Relationships Between Religious and Scientific Worldviews in the Narratives of Western Buddhists Reporting Meditation-Related Challenges," 2.

37 **"Today you have people":** Correspondence with the author via email, March 21, 2025. Emphasis in the original.

38 **But then you discover:** Jared Lindahl and Willoughby Britton, "'I Have This Feeling of Not Really Being Here': Buddhist Meditation and Changes in Sense of Self," *Journal of Consciousness Studies* 26:7–8 (2019): 157–83.

38 **Consider for a moment:** Lindahl and Britton, "'I Have This Feeling of Not Really Being Here,'" 10.

39 **In this text:** Bhikkhu Nanamoli and Bhikkhu Bodhi, trans., *The Middle Length Discourses of the Buddha: A New Translation of the Majjhima Nikaya* (Boston: Wisdom Publications, 1995), 145.

40 **In other words, they:** David McMahan, *Rethinking Meditation: Buddhist Meditative Practices in Ancient and Modern Worlds* (New York: Oxford University Press, 2023), 91.

41 **It began under:** David McMahan, "Buddhist Modernism," in *Buddhism in the Modern World* (New York: Taylor & Francis Group, 2012), 160.

41 **It is more accurate:** John Harding et al., "Introduction: Alternative Buddhist Modernities," *Journal of Global Buddhism* 21 (2002): 1–2.

42 **This allowed him:** McMahan, "Buddhist Modernism," 161, and Ann Gleig and Scott A. Mitchell, *The Oxford Handbook of American Buddhism* (New York: Oxford University Press, 2024).

42 **They presented Buddhism:** McMahan, "Buddhist Modernism," 162.

43 **In fact, in Theravada:** Patrick Pranke, "Vipassana," in *Encyclopedia of Buddhism*, vol. 2, ed. Robert Buswell (New York: Thomson Gale, 2004), 889–90.

43 **That included studying:** Erik Braun, *The Birth of Insight: Meditation, Modern Buddhism and Burmese Monk Ledi Sayadaw* (Chicago: University of Chicago Press, 2013), 4–6.

43 **According to Braun:** Braun, *The Birth of Insight*, 6.

44 **By the end of the week:** Bhante Gunaratana, *Journey to Mindfulness: The Autobiography of Bhante G* (Somerville, MA: Wisdom Publications, 2003/2017), 94.

45 **"When my friends heard":** Gunaratana, *Journey to Mindfulness,* 96.

45 **"Although I was well-versed":** Gunaratana, *Journey to Mindfulness,* 96.

45 **As Jeff Wilson:** Jeff Wilson, *Mindful America: The Mutual Transformation of Buddhist Meditation and America Culture* (New York: Oxford University Press, 2014), 76.

46 **While participating in:** Wilson, *Mindful America,* 85.

47 **Today, more than thirty thousand:** Stony Brook University, "Mindfulness Based Stress Reduction (MBSR) Courses," Healthier U Programs, https://www.stonybrook.edu/healthieru/programs/MBSR.

47 **which is offered:** MBSR Teachers Collaborative of Greater New York, "History of MBSR," https://mbsrcollaborative.com/history-of-mbsr.

47 **Kabat-Zinn said famously:** Wakoh Shannon Hickey, *Mind Cure: How Meditation Became Medicine* (New York: Oxford University Press, 2019), 138.

47 **As a white, non-Buddhist:** Jaime Kucinskas, *The Mindful Elite: Mobilizing from the Inside Out* (New York: Oxford University Press, 2019).

47 **"Reaction to TM":** Wilson, *Mindful America,* 80.

48 **Asian Buddhist modernist:** Ira Helderman, "Psychological Interpreters of Buddhism," *Oxford Research Encyclopedia of Religion,* April 30, 2020, https://oxfordre.com/religion/view/10.1093/acrefore/9780199340378.001.0001/acrefore-9780199340378-e-603.

48 **By the mid-twentieth century:** McMahan, "Buddhist Modernism," 168.

48 "Karma means": Jon Kabat-Zinn, *Wherever You Go, There You Are: Mindfulness and Meditation in Everyday Life* (New York: Hachette Books, 1994/2005/2023), 220.

49 When the Buddha: Wilson, *Mindful America*, 91.

51 "I undertake the precept to refrain": Access to Insight, "The Eight Precepts," The Barre Center of Buddhist Studies, https://www.accesstoinsight.org/ptf/dhamma/sila/atthasila.html.

52 "We find that because": Bhavana Society, "The Retreat Experience," https://bhavanasociety.org/retreats-and-events/the-retreat-experience/.

53 As Gajaweera describes it: Nalika Gajaweera, "'The more you give, the more will be yours to give': The Karmic Philanthropy of Kushil Gunasekera," *The Arrow*, May 18, 2021, https://arrow-journal.org/the-more-you-give-the-more-will-be-yours-to-give-the-karmic-philanthropy-of-kushil-gunasekera/.

53 Or as Kushil puts it: Gajaweera, "'The more you give, the more will be yours to give.'"

54 She concludes, "Indeed": Nalika Gajaweera, "Why Do Buddhists Give Money in Sri Lanka, but Not in the U.S.?," Center for Religion and Civic Culture, USC Dornsife, May 13, 2021, https://crcc.usc.edu/why-do-buddhists-give-money-in-sri-lanka-but-not-in-the-u-s/.

54 What makes sila/precepts: Gil Fronsdal, "The Curious Absence of the Precepts," *Inquiring Mind* 17.1 (Fall 2000), https://inquiringmind.com/article/1701_30_fronsdal_curious-absence-of-precepts/.

57 "Instead of the deep": Barry Magid and Marc Poirier, "The Three Shaky Pillars of Western Buddhism: Deracination, Secularization, and Instrumentalization," in *What's Wrong with Mindfulness (and What Isn't): Zen Perspectives*, ed. Robert Rosenbaum and Barry Magid (Somerville, MA: Wisdom Publications, 2016), 47.

57 They were developed within: Jared Lindahl et al., "The roles and impacts of worldviews in the context of meditation-related challenges," *Transcultural Psychiatry* 60.4 (2023): 645.

58 **He said that while:** Correspondence with the author via email, March 21, 2025.

58 **"Whereas members of the first":** Ann Gleig, *American Dharma: Buddhism Beyond Modernity* (New Haven, CT: Yale University Press, 2019), 175.

59 **Within a Buddhist worldview:** Gleig, *American Dharma,* 144.

59 **Mindfulness practice:** Nalika Gajaweera, "Sitting in the Fire Together: People of Color Cultivating Radical Resilience in North American Insight Meditation," *Journal of Global Buddhism* 22.1 (2021): 122.

59 **Eleanor Hancock, who developed:** Gleig, *American Dharma*, 150.

59 **"The practice is not":** Larry Yang, *Awakening Together: The Spiritual Practice of Inclusivity and Community* (Boston: Shambhala Publications, 2017), 130–31.

60 **This, she finds:** Nalika Gajaweera, "Sitting in the Fire Together," 122.

60 **"Since the invention":** Ira Helderman, "The McMindfulness Wars," *Tricycle: The Buddhist Review*, Fall 2021, https://tricycle.org/magazine/mcmindfulness-debate/

60 **In fact, Helderman writes:** Helderman, "The McMindfulness Wars."

60 **They hold up Buddhist:** Helderman, "The McMindfulness Wars."

CHAPTER 3: HIGHER POWER

65 **But in 1996:** *Griffin v. Coughlin*, 88 N.Y.2d 674 at 683.

66 **"Alcoholics Anonymous does not":** Alcoholics Anonymous, *Twelve Steps and Twelve Traditions* (New York: Alcoholics Anonymous Publishing, 1952), 26.

67 **And it was through:** Alcoholics Anonymous, *Alcoholics Anonymous: The Story of How Many Thousands of Men and Women Have Recovered from Alcoholism* (aka *The Big Book*) (Alcoholics Anonymous World Services, Inc., 1939), 9.

67 **"Last summer an alcoholic":** Alcoholics Anonymous, *The Big Book*, 9.

67 **He distrusted organized religion:** Alcoholics Anonymous, *The Big Book*, 11.

67 **"Why don't you choose":** Alcoholics Anonymous, *The Big Book*, 12.

68 **Here are the Twelve Steps:** Alcoholics Anonymous, *Twelve Steps and Twelve Traditions*, 5–8.

70 **He begins . . . by sharing:** Alcoholics Anonymous, *The Big Book*, 45.

70 **"We found that":** Alcoholics Anonymous, *The Big Book*, 46.

70 **A 2023 survey:** Becka Alper et al., "Spirituality Among Americans," Pew Research Center, December 7, 2023, https://www.pewresearch.org/religion/2023/12/07/spirituality-among-americans/.

71 **His wife had left him:** Alcoholics Anonymous, *The Big Book*, 219.

71 **His first impression:** Alcoholics Anonymous, *The Big Book*, 227.

71 **"I was a menace":** Alcoholics Anonymous, *The Big Book*, 227.

71 **During meetings, while everyone:** Alcoholics Anonymous, *The Big Book*, 228.

71 **"*I* was all right":** Alcoholics Anonymous, *The Big Book*, 227.

71 **As he tells it:** Alcoholics Anonymous, *The Big Book*, 227.

72 **During a work lunch:** Alcoholics Anonymous, *The Big Book*, 228.

72 **"My brilliant agnosticism":** Alcoholics Anonymous, *The Big Book*, 229.

72 **In that respect:** Alcoholics Anonymous, *Twelve Steps and Twelve Traditions*, 27.

72 **In an article titled:** Jim Burwell, "Sober for Thirty Years," *A.A. Grapevine*, May 1968.

73 **As historian Ernest Kurtz:** Ernest Kurtz, *Not-God: A History of Alcoholics Anonymous* (Center City, MN: Hazelden, 1979, 1991), 3.

74 **And legally speaking:** See *Lynch v. Donnelly* 465 US 668 (1983) at 683.

77 **"We admitted we were":** Al-Anon Family Groups, *Paths to Recovery: Al-Anon's Steps, Traditions, and Concepts* (Virginia Beach, VA: Al-Anon Family Group Headquarters, 1997), 7.

77 **In the first section:** Al-Anon Family Groups, *Paths to Recovery*, 8.

77 **"It took time":** Al-Anon Family Groups, *Paths to Recovery*, 13.

83 **A 2000 study:** Monica Hortsmann and J. Scott Tonigan, "Faith Development in Alcoholics Anonymous (AA)," Alcoholism Treatment Quarterly 18.4 (2000): 80.

83 **Several other studies:** For example, K. Matzgeret et al., "Reasons for drinking less and their relationship to sustained remission from problem drinking," *Addiction* 100.11 (2005): 1637–46; Stephen Strobbe et al., "Spiritual Awakening Predicts Improved Drinking Outcomes in a Polish Treatment Sample," *Journal of Addictions Nursing* 24.4 (2013): 215; and Alyssa Forchehimes, "De Profundis: Spiritual Transformations in Alcoholics Anonymous," *Journal of Clinical Psychology: In Session* 60.5 (2004): 504.

83 ***The Big Book* assures us:** Alcoholics Anonymous, *The Big Book*, 567.

84 **"I feel my spiritual":** Burwell, "Sober for Thirty Years."

84 **"Most of us think":** Alcoholics Anonymous, *The Big Book*, 568.

85 **"In belaboring the sins":** Alcoholics Anonymous, *Twelve Steps and Twelve Traditions*, 30.

CHAPTER 4: EATING WELL

88 **This food plan:** Will Cole, "Gwyneth Paltrow: Her Wellness Protocol for Longevity and Gut Health, Keyboard Warriors . . . ," *The Art of Being Well with Dr. Will Cole*, Episode 169, March 13, 2023.

88 **It is linked:** National Eating Disorders Association, "Health Consequences," reviewed by Kim Dennis, MD, CEDS, https://www.nationaleatingdisorders.org/health-consequences/.

88 **And eating disorders:** Jon Arcelus et al., "Mortality rates in patients with anorexia nervosa and other eating disorders. A meta-analysis of 36 studies," *Archives of General Psychiatry* 68.7 (2011): 724–31.

89 **Nine percent of the U.S.:** Deloitte Access Economics, *The Social and Economic Cost of Eating Disorders in the United States of America: A Report for the Strategic Training Initiative for the Prevention of Eating Disorders and the Academy for Eating Disorders*, June 2000, https://www.deloitte.com/au/en/services/economics/perspectives/social-economic-cost-eating-disorders-united-states.html.

89 **Although eating disorders are assumed:** Deloitte Access Economics, *The Social and Economic Cost of Eating Disorders in the United States of America*.

89 **This lets him feel:** Jeff Haden, "While Twitter CEO Jack Dorsey Eats Only 1 Meal a Day (and Even Just 5 Per Week)," *Inc.*, April 11, 2019, https://www.inc.com/jeff-haden/while-twitter-ceo-jack-dorsey-eats-just-1-meal-a-day-sometimes-only-5-per-week-heres-what-you-really-should-know-about-intermittent-fasting.html.

92 **Augustine, for instance:** Augustine of Hippo, *City of God*, book 14 (New York: Penguin Classics, 2004).

92 **Tertullian, a prolific Christian:** Hannah Bacon, "Fat, Syn, and Disordered Eating: The Dangers and Powers of Excess," *Fat Studies* 4 (2015): 93.

92 **In the fifth century:** Bacon, "Fat, Syn, and Disordered Eating," 92.

92 **Here the goal was:** Caroline Walker Bynum, *Holy Feast and Holy Fast* (Berkeley: University of California Press, 1987).

93 **In 1970, Pope Paul VI:** The Editors of Encyclopaedia Britannica, "Doctor of the Church," *Encyclopedia Britannica*, https://www.britannica.com/topic/Doctor-of-the-Church.

94 **"Eating was the one thing":** Interview by author, April 15, 2025.

94 **What Melanie had in common:** Joan Jacobs Brumberg, *Fasting Girls: The History of Anorexia Nervosa* (New York: Vintage Books, 1988, 2000), 10.

94 **"The anorectic is refusing":** Joanne Woolway Grenfell, "Religion and Eating Disorders: Towards Understanding a Neglected Perspective," *Feminist Theology* 14.3 (2006): 373.

95 **"They were like":** Interview by author, April 15, 2025.

96 **"Shoes are dirty not in themselves":** Mary Douglas, *Purity and Danger: An Analysis of Concepts of Pollution and Taboo* (London: Psychology Press, 2003), 38.

97 **As nutritionist Karen Reyes:** As quoted in Victoria Stokes, "Gwyneth Paltrow: Why Some Experts Label Her Restrictive Diet as 'Disordered Eating,'" *Healthline*, March 21, 2023, https://www.healthline.com/health-news/gwyneth-paltrow-restrictive-diet-criticism.

97 **This is presented as the result:** Food Babe, "My Visit to the White House—Exposing Big Food and Advocating Major Food Chemical Reform," https://foodbabe.com/my-visit-to-the-white-house-exposing-big-food-and-advocating-major-food-chemical-reform/.

97 **Raw milk has harmful:** FDA, "The Dangers of Raw Milk: Unpasteurized Milk Can Pose a Serious Health Risk," May 20, 2024, https://www.fda.gov/food/buy-store-serve-safe-food/dangers-raw-milk-unpasteurized-milk-can-pose-serious-health-risk.

97 **"The renunciation":** Susannah Crockford, *Ripples of the Universe: Spirituality in Sedona* (Chicago: University of Chicago Press, 2021), 133.

98 **By the twentieth century:** R. Marie Griffiths, "'Don't Eat That': The Erotics of Abstinence in American Christianity," *Gastronomica* 1.4 (Fall 2001): 37.

98 **"The scriptures and understanding":** Griffiths, "'Don't Eat That.'"

99 **Just as God rescued:** Gwen Shamblin, *The Weigh Down Diet: Inspirational Way to Lose Weight, Stay Slim and Find a New You* (New York: Doubleday, 1997), 11.

99 **"Fat people don't go":** Shamblin as quoted in "Fat People Don't Go to Heaven," *Globe*, November 21, 2000.

99 **Thinness was a sign:** Interview with author, April 15, 2025.

104 **For instance, in a 2021 article:** Archana Purushotham and Alex Hankey, "Vegetarian Diets, Ayurveda, and the Case for an Integrative Nutrition Science," *Medicina* 57.858 (2021): 1–5, https://doi.org/10.3390/medicina57090858.

105 **The first was a massive:** T. Y. N. Tong et al., "Risks of ischaemic heart disease and stroke in meat eaters, fish eaters, and vegetarians over 18 years of follow-up: Results from the prospective EPIC-Oxford study," *BMJ* 366 (2019): 14897.

105 **By contrast, a separate study:** T. H. T. Chiu, H. R. Chang, L. Y. Wang, et al., "Vegetarian diet and incidence of total, ischemic, and hemorrhagic stroke in 2 cohorts in Taiwan," *Neurology* (March 17, 2020): e1112–e1121, https://www.ncbi.nlm.nih.gov/pmc/articles/PMC7220235/pdf/NEUROLOGY2019979377.pdf.

105 **"In general, legumes":** Purushotham and Hankey, "Vegetarian Diets, Ayurveda, and the Case for an Integrative Nutrition Science," 3.

106 **"You who believe":** The Qur'an: A New Translation by M.A.S. Abdel Haleem (New York: Oxford University Press, 2004).

107 **"God wants ease":** The Qur'an: A New Translation by M.A.S. Abdel Haleem.

108 **"If somebody is trying":** David DeSteno, host, "Fasting for the Soul," *How God Works: The Science Behind Spirituality*, PRX (April 20, 2025), 7:20.

108 **If you're fasting:** DeSteno, "Fasting for the Soul," 7:35.

108 **Researchers hypothesized:** Merve Balkaya-Ince et al., "Does Ramadan serve as a naturalistic intervention to promote Muslim American adolescents' daily virtues? Evidence from a three wave experience sampling study," *The Journal of Positive Psychology* 19.5 (2024): 811.

108 **"We sit together":** Zahra Alghafli et al., "A Qualitative Study of Ramadan: A Month of Fasting, Family, and Faith," *Religions* 10.123 (2019): 9.

110 **"It is clear":** Al-Ghazali, *The Mysteries of Fasting*, trans. Nabih Amin Faris (Lahore: Sh. Muhammad Ashraf Publishers, 1992), 32.

110 **For those further along:** Fareeha Jay, "Ramadan and eating disorders," BDA: The Association of UK Dietitians, April 6, 2022, https://www.bda.uk.com/resource/ramadan-and-eating-disorders.html.

111 **"A lot of times":** Rania Awaad, interview with the author, April 26, 2025.

111 **An eating disorder, she writes:** Omara Naseem, *Ramadan and Eating Disorder Guide*, 5, https://omaranaseem.com/wp-content/uploads/2022/04/Ramadan-and-Eating-Disorder-Guide-Dr-Naseem_V3.pdf.

112 **In more acute cases:** Rania Awaad, interview with the author, April 26, 2025.

112 **"Risking one's health":** Rania Awaad, "Eating Disorders and Ramadan: Debunking the Myths, Mechanisms to Cope," *Muslim Matters*, March 24, 2023, https://muslimmatters.org/2023/03/24/eating-disorder-and-ramadan-debunking-the-myths-mechanisms-to-cope/.

112 **"There's a hadith":** Interview with the author, April 24, 2025. Sahih al-Bukhari, book 67, Hadith 133, narrated by 'Abdullah bin Umr bin al-'As, https://sunnah.com/bukhari:5199.

113 **The moral question is not:** Jacques Derrida, "'Eating Well,' or the Calculation of the Subject: An Interview with Jacques Derrida," in *Who Comes After the Subject*, ed. Eduardo Cadava et al. (New York: Routledge, 1991), 115.

114 **This is why:** Marie Dallam, "Introduction: Religion, Food, and Eating," in *Religion, Food, and Eating in North America*, ed. Benjamin Zeller et al. (New York: Columbia University Press, 2014), xviii.

114 **Preparing food, she says:** Elizabeth Pérez, *Religion in the Kitchen: Cooking, Talking, and the Making of Black Atlantic Traditions* (New York: New York University Press, 2016), 9.

CHAPTER 5: SPIRITUAL FITNESS

118 **"Whoever you are":** https://www.soul-cycle.com/soulconnected/soulcycle-sanctuary-manifesto/.

119 **A friend who is also:** I won't include names of any of the former instructors I spoke to because they had all signed nondisclosure agreements.

122 **This is when we see:** James Whorton, *Crusaders for Fitness: The History of American Health Reformers* (Princeton, NJ: Princeton University Press, 1982).

122 **Advocates of muscular Christianity:** See a brief discussion of women and exercise in mid-nineteenth century in Harvey

Green, *Fit for America* (Baltimore, MD: The Johns Hopkins University Press, 1986), 184–85.

124 **To Quimby, they were examples:** Wakoh Shannon Hickey, *Mind Cure: How Meditation Became Medicine* (Oxford: Oxford University Press, 2019), 34-36.

126 **He acknowledges those:** M. Weber, *Economy and Society* (Berkeley: University of California Press, 1978), 1112.

128 **"All my years":** Stacey Griffith, *Two Turns from Zero* (New York: William Morrow, 2017), 53.

131 **And there were also "religious versions":** PraiseMoves .com, accessed September 23, 2025, https://praisemoves.com.

133 **When she reached 212 pounds:** Patricia Moreno's April 10, 2018, email "Has anyone noticed that it's not working?" sent to the intenSati community.

133 **"I loved dance":** Patricia Moreno's April 10, 2018, email "Has anyone noticed that it's not working?" sent to intenSati community.

133 **"I was muscular":** *intenSati Teacher Training Manual*, 22.

134 **She read best-selling:** *intenSati Teacher Training Manual*, 23.

134 **"That's it!":** *intenSati Teacher Training Manual*, 24.

134 **"If people are crying":** Interview by Rose Surnow, "Love, Sweat and Tears: Intensati Kicks Your Ass and Cleanses Your Soul," *Cosmopolitan*, July 16, 2013.

136 **"I was getting better":** Interview with the author, January 17, 2025.

136 **"6 foot tall Mexican-American":** Interview with the author, January 17, 2025.

137 **"He was the embodiment":** Interview with the author, December 17, 2024.

137 **"To be honest with you":** Interview with the author, December 17, 2024.

138 **"I immediately had that feeling":** Interview with the author, December 17, 2024.

138 **By the time:** Lucy Osborne correspondence with the author via email, January 29, 2025.

139 **As Osborne put it:** Lucy Osborne correspondence with the author via email, April 2, 2025.

140 **"Your introduction":** Lucy Osborne correspondence with the author via email, April 2, 2025.

142 **Tears were streaming down:** "intenSati LIVE with Lucy Osborne—Divine Guidance," January 29, 2022, https://vimeo.com/671572355/0afe41d72c.

CHAPTER 6: DEEP LISTENING

146 **"If meditation is taking":** As quoted by Nicole Dellert and Emily Rekstis, "What Is a Sound Bath? Experts Explain the Meditation's Origins and Benefits," *Allure*, February 21, 2023.

149 **Most important for this chapter:** Judith Becker, *Deep Listeners: Music, Emotion, and Trancing* (Bloomington: Indiana University Press, 2004), 1.

149 **That study of sixty-two:** Tamara L. Goldsby et al., "Effects of Singing Bowl Sound Meditation on Mood, Tension, and Well-Being: An Observational Study," *Journal of Evidence-Based Complementary and Alternative Medicine* 22.3 (2017): 401–6.

150 **Jayan Marie Landry:** Jayan Marie Landry, "Physiological and Psychological Effects of a Himalayan Singing Bowl in Meditation Practice: A Quantitative Analysis," *American Journal of Health Promotion* 28.5 (2014): 306–9.

150 **Some posit that sound:** Ik-Soo Ann and Myungjin Bae, "Analysis of Singing Bowl's Sound," *The Journal of the Acoustical Society of America* 142 (2017): 2613.

150 **Others think the effects:** Peter Goodwin, Joseph Ciorciari, Kate Baker, et al., "A High-Density EEG Investigation into Steady State Binaural Beat Stimulation," *PLoS One* 7: e34789.

150 **And still others suggest:** Gudrun Agusta Sigurdardottir, Peter Michael Nielsen, Jesper Ronager, and August Gabriel Wang, "A pilot study of high amplitude low frequency-music impulse stimulation as an add-on treatment for depression," *Brain and Behavior* 9 (2019): e01399.

150 **Underlying all these theories:** Ted Gioia, *Healing Songs* (Durham, NC: Duke University Press, 2006), 10.

152 **Their role as sacred:** Ben Joffe, "Tripping on Good Vibrations: Cultural Commodification and Tibetan Singing Bowls," *Savage Minds*, October 31, 2015.

152 **He thinks enterprising:** Robert Barnett, "Understated Legacies: Uses of Oral History and Tibetan Studies," *Inner Asia* 12 (2010): 63–93.

152 **Instead of searching:** Becker, *Deep Listeners*, 2.

154 **According to Durkheim, when we gather:** Émile Durkheim, *The Elementary Forms of Religious Life*, trans. J. D. Swan (London: George Allen & Unwin, 1912/1915), 215–16.

154 **A result of "emitting same cries":** Durkheim, *The Elementary Forms of Religious Life,* 212.

156 **For instance, an often-cited:** Goldsby et al., "Effects of Singing Bowl Sound Meditation on Mood, Tension, and Well-Being," 401–4.

158 **Getting the full benefits:** Bhai Gurcharan Singh, *Kirtan Nirmolak Heera and the Art of Music* (New Delhi: Gurmat Printing Press, 2008), 58.

159 **To learn more:** Raja Academy website, "About," https://rajacademy.com/about.

159 **"We are 'feeling' beings":** Raja Academy website, "About."

160 **"Active listening is something":** SikhNet, "The Benefits of Kirtan," https://www.sikhnet.com/news/benefits-kirtan.

161 **He thought those big feelings:** Durkheim, *The Elementary Forms of Religious Life*, 427.

161 If he was right: Durkheim, *The Elementary Forms of Religious Life,* 210–11.

162 But listening with attention: Charles Hirschkind, *The Ethical Soundscape: Cassette Sermons and Islamic Counterpublics* (New York: Columbia University Press, 2006), 70.

162 "Things must not stop": Hirschkind, *The Ethical Soundscape,* 92.

162 Hirschkind argues that: Hirschkind, *The Ethical Soundscape,* 74.

163 It depends on: Hirschkind, *The Ethical Soundscape,* 75.

163 Judith Becker, author: Becker, *Deep Listeners,* 151.

164 Alexandre Tannous, an ethnomusicologist: Alexandre Tannous, "Trading Our Chains for Enchantment," Sound Meditation, https://soundmeditation.com/trading-our-chains-for-enchantment/.

CHAPTER 7: PSYCHEDELIC SACRAMENTS

168 Studies out of universities: See, for example, Natalie Gukasyan et al., "Efficacy and safety of psilocybin-assisted treatment for major depressive disorder: Prospective 12-month follow-up," *Journal of Psychopharmacology* 36.2 (2022): 151–58.

168 Some of these trials: See, for example, R. R. Griffiths et al., "Psilocybin can occasion mystical-type experiences having substantial and sustained personal meaning and spiritual significance," *Psychopharmacology* 187 (2006): 268–83.

169 After a 1957: Gordon Wasson, "Seeking the Magic Mushroom," *Life,* May 13, 1957, 100–120.

170 This means "seemingly benign": Diana Negrín, "Colonial Shadows in the Psychedelic Renaissance," in *Psychedelic Justice: Toward a Diverse and Equitable Psychedelic Culture,* eds. Beatriz Caiuby Labate and Clancy Cavnar (Boulder, CO: University of Colorado Boulder, 2021), 41.

174 **Mike Crowley, a psychedelically inclined:** Mike Crowley, *Secret Drugs of Buddhism: Psychedelic Sacraments and the Origins of the Vajrayana* (Santa Fe, NM: Synergetic Press, 2019), 183.

174 **The ancient Greek lyric poet:** Robert Forte, *Entheogens and the Future of Religion* (San Francisco: Council on Spiritual Practices, 2000), 33.

174 **The famous Roman philosopher:** Forte, *Entheogens and the Future of Religion,* 92.

177 **Santo Daime is quite similar:** *Church of the Holy Light of the Queen v. Mukasey,* United States District Court, D. Oregon, March 18, 2009.

179 **"For as long as I can remember":** Huston Smith, *Cleansing the Doors of Perception: The Religious Significance of Entheogenic Plants and Chemicals* (New York: Sentient Publications, 2000), 100–101.

179 **In a 1964 essay:** Smith, *Cleansing the Doors of Perception,* 30.

182 **"By drinking the Daime":** G. William Barnard, *Liquid Light: Ayahuasca Spirituality and the Santo Daime Tradition* (New York: Columbia University Press, 2022), 242.

185 **"To be a medium":** Jonathan Goldman, *Gift of the Body* (Bend, OR: Essential Light Institute, 2014), 209.

185 **We all have the potential:** Goldman, *Gift of the Body,* 209.

188 **At the time I had no idea:** Goldman, *Gift of the Body,* 237.

192 **Psychedelics, administered in:** David Marchese, "A Psychedelics Pioneer Takes the Ultimate Trip," *The New York Times Magazine*, April 7, 2003, https://www.nytimes.com/interactive/2023/04/03/magazine/roland-griffiths-interview.html.

192 **The key, Griffiths thought:** Marchese, "A Psychedelics Pioneer Takes the Ultimate Trip."

194 **And that gravitas:** As quoted by Don Lattin, *God on Psychedelics: Tripping Across the Rubble of Old-Time Religion* (Hannacroix, NY: The Apocryphile Press, 2023), 40.

194 **As Green puts it:** As quoted by Don Lattin, *God on Psychedelics*, 40.

195 **This is the real purpose:** Huston Smith attributes this phrase to Robert Ornstein. Smith, *Cleansing the Doors of Perception*, 153.

Index

About the Author

LIZ BUCAR is a religious ethicist and professor of religion at Northeastern University, as well as a certified intenSati and Kripalu yoga instructor. Her popular writing has appeared in *The Atlantic*, the *Los Angeles Times*, *Teen Vogue*, and *The Wall Street Journal*, and she is the author of four academic books, including the award-winning *Stealing My Religion* and *Pious Fashion*. She lives in Brookline, Massachusetts. For more about how religion shapes us all, even if we don't believe, subscribe to Liz's newsletter at lizbucar.com.